Infinite

HAPPINESS

MASAMI SAIONJI is descended from the
Royal Ryukyu Family of Okinawa. She is
the Chairperson of The World Peace Prayer
Society, an international organization based
in New York, and The Byakko Shinko Kai,
founded in Japan.

by the same author

THE GOLDEN KEY TO HAPPINESS

Infinite HAPPINESS

Discovering Your Inner Wisdom

MASAMI SAIONJI

ELEMENT

Shaftesbury, Dorset • Rockport, Massachusetts
Brisbane, Queensland

Text © Masami Saionji 1996

First published in Great Britain in 1996 by
Element Books Limited
Shaftesbury, Dorset SP7 8BP

Published in the USA in 1996 by
Element Books, Inc.
PO Box 830, Rockport, MA 01966

Published in Australia in 1996 by
Element Books Limited for
Jacaranda Wiley Limited
33 Park Road, Milton, Brisbane 4064

Translated by Kinuko Hamaya, Seiji Hashimoto, Mako Ishibashi,
Shoko Kawano, Masami Kondo, Mary McQuaid and Kyoko Selden,
with special thanks to Robert G. Saphier.

Edited by E. Glyn Davies

Text design/composition by Paperwork, Ithaca, New York
Cover design by Max Fairbrother
Printed and bound in Great Britain by Biddles Ltd, Guildford &
Kings Lynn.

British Library Cataloguing in Publication data available
Library of Congress Cataloging in Publication data available

ISBN 1-85230-885-0

CONTENTS

PREFACE

When I started writing this book, I had one clear purpose in mind. I strongly wished to help people let go of their deeply rooted attachments to suffering and misery, so that they might free up their energy for creating a peaceful and happy life.

Many people think that happiness cannot be won without fighting and struggling for it. Others believe that to earn happiness, they must somehow prove themselves worthy of it.

I would like you to know that to attain happiness, you need not go through harsh discipline, sacrifice or strain. Nor do you need long years of study, struggle or endurance. Simply by reading this book, I believe that you can naturally start to rediscover the abundantly overflowing happiness and health that already exist within you.

As you read each page, I pray that the words will leap into your heart, becoming a source of light and energy to activate your life. One after another, may they spark off a wondrous, inner transformation, bringing you face to face with a glorious new 'you'.

Once this transformation has taken place, you will see that there is no need at all for you to follow anyone else, struggle with anyone else, or seek happiness from anyone else. With your own strength, your own power and your own infinitely shining energy, you will freely create your own wonderful endless life.

May bright courage always well up within you, guiding you and mankind toward a rich and harmonious future.

MASAMI SAIONJI

Chapter 1

THE WORLDS THAT
WE ARE CREATING

One by one, each of us forms mankind on the planet earth. There is a world where you are. It exists because of you. In fact, you are creating it, right now. You are its sole creator.

While creating the world of mankind and the world of society, people also create their own worlds around them. Each world is created by the way a person thinks. Your thought, alone, determines whether you create a peaceful world or a tragic world, a rich, harmonious world or a desolate world.

Even if members of a family live under the same roof, each of them lives in a separate world. Though you live in the same building, share the same space and eat the same food, you never live in the same world. Each of you builds your own, individual world to live in, for each of you has your own way of thinking, different from others'.

If your family is closely knit by a bond of blood, you might think that you live in the same world, but it cannot be so. Different members of a family live in entirely different worlds: the children could be living in heaven while their parents are living on earth.

Yet you believe that you and your family live in the same world. How could husband and wife or parent and child live in the same world when their thoughts are different? People live in the world their thoughts create. They cannot leave that world, nor can others live in the world that you are creating with your thought.

Once you have settled into your world, the same world forms itself around you wherever you go. It can do no other, since it is your world. You can communicate your thoughts, experiences and way of living to your marriage partner or your child, but that is as far as it goes. You can never guide the other along the path of your own thinking, for your spouse and your child create their own worlds with their own thought.

⁀ How Can We Change Our World?

If you wish to rescue your children from a hellish world of their own creation, you must first guide them in a way that allows them to change their thinking, for your children's thought supplies the energy that creates that kind of world.

Everyone lives in the world of their own thought. If the society around them is miserable and corrupt, most people think that they must start by changing society – but this is a mistake. No one is capable of changing others, nor is there any reason to think that anyone should be able to. Though you may try to change your husband, wife, parent or child, in the end you will never really be able to.

If you truly wish to leave the world you live in, you must start by changing your thought. Unless you first make a change in your thought, you will not find a way out of your world.

The same is true for your loved ones. If your beloved parent or child is unhappy, if your dear brother or sister is in misery, the responsibility does not lie with anyone else. Their situation arises from their own way of thinking, their own wishes and feelings.

Suppose you dislike the world you live in. You might leave your home or run away from society, but your world will follow after you. Even if you succeed in placing yourself in a new environment, you will not be able to run away from the 'self' that you created. How could you run away from your own self?

Wherever you might hide, you would always end up creating the same world again, just like before.

Why should your world turn out the same as before? It is because your thought has not changed. If you are determined to change your world, you must change your way of thinking. The moment you do that, a totally different world will take shape around you.

If your thoughts are truthful, the world you create will be truthful. If you live with a desire for things that have no substance, you will create a world of falsity and pretension. In every sense, the 'self' that you create projects itself through the world around you. And since no two people have exactly the same thoughts, the number of worlds on earth is exactly the same as the number of people.

Even when we depart from this earthly world, we cannot leave the worlds that we are creating. Wherever we go, each of us keeps building our own world around us. Each world is newly created, moment by moment, by the way a person thinks.

✑ Who is Responsible for a Child's Destiny?

Of late, the troubles between parents and children seem unending. Parents continually worry when their children do not smoothly progress as they are expected to.

Parents see their children beset by all sorts of physical and emotional problems. While parents can endure their own difficulties, the sight of their children's unhappiness is excruciatingly painful for them. When they see their children suffering from various problems, most parents acutely feel that it is their own responsibility, and they blame and judge themselves for their inadequacy.

If children could experience wonderful improvements because their parents blamed themselves over and over again, it would be an excellent thing to do. But this almost never happens. If, by holding themselves responsible and condemning themselves for their children's misfortunes, they could make their children get better, all parents ought to blame and judge themselves from head to toe. But the reality is that parental self-blame, however extensive, can hardly bring an improvement in children.

The suffering and misfortune that children carry is never the fault of their parents, nor is it the parents' responsibility. It is the outcome of the children's own wishes, the precise manifestation of their own thought and behaviour. This can be said about very young children, or even tiny infants only a few months old.

Not knowing the true principle behind this, how many parents go on lamenting and grieving to no avail? How many of them consume their days pouring all their energy into their children, and end their years with a dark and wretched feeling in their hearts?

✑ Tune in to Truth

What makes the truth so hard to understand? The absolute truth inevitably becomes distorted when it passes through this material world. It is just like putting a straight stick into water. The stick remains straight, yet it looks bent because a refraction is produced through the medium of the water. Mentally, we know very well that the stick is straight, yet the physical eye perceives it in bent form.

This is exactly what happens to truth. Though truth is magnificently straight, it looks bent when it passes through the medium called the physical body, the medium called society, or the medium known as worldly common sense. When truth passes through the medium of thought, it becomes warped – forcefully bent. Truth is no longer truth.

And so, when seen through the medium of worldly common sense, it appears that children are wholly the responsibility of their parents. Everything that concerns the child is deflected to the parents.

Certainly, parents have a duty to amply protect, nurture

and bring up little children. However, as children rapidly grow, they begin to have their own opinions, their own will. At that point, we cannot say that they are wholly the parents' responsibility. Their lives are now reflecting their own inborn traits, character and talent, as well as the habits they have brought with them from past worlds. Their lives now reflect their own thought.

Who can step into a child's mind? Not even a parent can. No one is allowed to trespass there, and it would be unspeakably arrogant for parents to think that they could change their children's thoughts and feelings. No parent has that right, for children, like adults, shape their own lives with their own free will.

A parent is never more than a guide. If you can point out the way that leads to truth – to the child's divinity – that alone is enough. If the child rejects your guidance, or even heads in the reverse direction, let it be, for this is your child's chosen way. In this lifetime, there are things children must attempt on their own. A rugged path may await them, yet once they reconcile the debts that followed them to this world, a wonderful, shining future will span out for them when they advance to the next.

This is one of the ways that the soul grows and matures. It is one step in a child's learning process. It is truly foolish to torment yourself over the ups and downs of your child's present way of living, for you are merely glimpsing a short scene in the child's endless life.

When you see your child suffering, the misery might seem so relentless that you wish you could take on even a little of it in his or her place. It is understandable that you feel this way. Yet the truth is that you are only indulging your own emotions. You are not helping the child.

✎ *Pray for the Child's Divine Missions*

If you truly love your children and want what is best for them, pray that they will successfully go through the things that they must go through. This is the only thing you can do. Even if you were allowed to bear part of your children's burden on their behalf, sooner or later the same pain and misery would await them once more. They would not have been spared their suffering; it would merely have been postponed. If children do not fulfil the tasks assigned to them during this lifetime, later on they will again find themselves in the very same kind of world.

Parents, I ask that you be stern, even if you feel like an ogre at times. Your child is the only one who can fulfil your child's destiny.[1] It is there to polish their soul. It is a process that will make them worthy and accomplished. It is a path that will prepare them to walk freely in the way of truth. Understand this well: though your child's anguish may seem severe, it can be overcome by the child alone. It cannot be resolved by you, the parent.

Why must you be upset and confused?

Why must you torment yourself?

Why must you feel that you are responsible?

Why must you assume a burden that is not yours?

Why must you throw your life into chaos on account of the child, even entangling the destinies of the sisters and brothers around him or her?

All the conditions that surround the child are there for the child. The child is the one who must take care of them. That is why the child has drawn them to himself or herself. If you are the one who suffers from those conditions, feeling that you are at fault, you are mistaken. It was the child who attracted those things, not you.

Suffer no more for your child's fate. Resent it no more. Anger yourself no more. Struggle no more against your child's misery. Your suffering is useless. Your anger, your resentment and your struggling are useless, because it was not you who invited the child's fate: it was the child. Everything around the child arose from the child's own thinking. If you strongly feel responsible, you are not helping the child – you are standing in the way of his or her spiritual progress.

Each child's birth was arranged at a certain time and place so that they could accomplish the tasks that awaited them and clear away the debts previously incurred by their soul. If you deeply love the child, simply pray for him or her without saying a word. Pray that the child will waken to truth even one day sooner.

The two of you share a link from the past that brought you together in this world as parent and child. Through this link, when you pray for the God-given missions of the child that you love, you can rest assured that, in some way, the truth will be conveyed to him or her. Eventually, the child will wake. Once the child's thoughts change, his or her painful world will be transformed.

Relinquish Your Attachments

Parents, give up your attachment to your children. Attachment brings pain and anguish. Nothing encumbers a child more than parental attachment. Once an attachment has been formed, it does not know where to stop. Let things be as they are. If you leave trouble alone, it will leave you of its own accord. Do not pull it toward you forcefully. Follow the nature of things and the nature of yourself.

Attachment comes from not knowing the truth, and it is the very thing that keeps us from the truth. People attach themselves to love, to hatred, to sadness and to joy. They attach themselves to the past, and also to the future. They attach themselves to material things, to social status and to authority. They attach themselves to their husbands, wives and children, to land, property or riches. Once they attach themselves to something, their attachment knows no limits.

Whatever you do, it is important that your mind be free. When you attach yourself to something, everything comes to a standstill. Your energy stops flowing; it fixes itself in one spot.

Human beings are meant to be absolutely free – not

caught up in anything. Attaching yourself to something is like binding yourself with fetters. You should be praised if you can refrain from attaching yourself to anything – even more so if you can be that way about the children that you love. When you have released your attachments, your mind will be freed from suffering.

When you stop attaching yourself to the things and events going on around you, you will no longer draw problems toward you. At that moment your children, freed from the burden of your attachment, will suddenly begin to shine with life's energy.

A great many people have formed deep attachments to unhappiness. No sooner do they extricate themselves from one misfortune than they quickly catch hold of another. To me it looks as though they harbour an inner yearning for misfortune. I cannot help thinking that, in their hearts, they enjoy advertising their unhappiness to others.

Their misfortunes are perhaps their most cherished treasures. By creating new misfortunes one after another, it could be that they are trying to bring meaning and purpose to their lives.

Spend Your Energy Well

Why do miseries keep occurring in your heart? It is because you continue to support their existence. Without your support, not one of them could survive. They exist precisely because you keep giving energy to them. No one forces you to do that.

It takes energy to be sad. Without using our energy, we cannot lament and grieve. In order to create sorrow and affliction, we must constantly put forth the appropriate amount of energy.

People are spending enormous energy on things with no value or meaning at all. They have worn themselves out from having spent so much energy on anger and sorrow. They have used up even the energy needed to recover from those things. They heedlessly squander their energy as they walk along their self-created path to ruin. This is pure folly, nothing more.

Every self-negating thought requires energy. Gloomy thoughts, sad thoughts, depressing thoughts – all these require tremendous quantities of energy. In order to sustain and perpetuate your thinking, you can rely only on the energy that is within you, energy that is not provided to you by anyone else. When you use up your energy in creating dark thoughts, you are chipping away at the energy that supports your own life. This is an utter waste of your most precious treasure.

Conversely, all positive thinking works like a generator of energy, causing more and more new energy to surge forth. When you live trying to turn everything toward the positive, your thoughts and feelings radiate light, becoming a source of life. Far from diminishing your life-energy, they newly regenerate your unlimited potential, time and time again.

A light-oriented lifestyle generates infinite vitality, infinite love, health and happiness. Everything renews itself and comes alive with resplendent energy and power.

You Choose Where to Focus Your Energy

It is not difficult to live a light-oriented lifestyle. You are only making it difficult by thinking that it is difficult. Just keep facing the bright light of your inner Self. Keep attuning yourself to it.

You need not try to look like a good person. That will only turn you into a hypocrite. If the truth were known, there are times when people wish to be good and upright without making any real effort in that direction – simply because all they really want is to tell themselves that they are good and upright people, and to be thought of that way by others.

Here is how you wield your energy to manifest your thought: first, you wish for something; next, the image of your desire takes shape in your mind; then you keep sending your energy toward that image, again and again. You continue to send your energy toward it until your desire manifests itself in your world.

This is truly a wondrous function. Though no orders are

issued, the process naturally works on its own as you direct your energy toward various goals that you determine with your thought.

For example, if you spend a lot of energy thinking about misery and failure, misery and failure come into view, and you project misery and failure into the world that you are creating. Conversely, if you focus all your attention on the limitless divine love and power that are within you, unlimited love and power are drawn out and projected wherever you wish.

Our destinies are shaped in this way. Depending on how we focus our energy, we can walk the way of misfortune or create a world of happiness. The decision is ours alone.

Graduate From Your Circumstances

Either through a link from the past or else for some divine purpose, two people are brought together in this world as parent and child. Even so, a parent has to progress along his or her own path in life, and that path is determined by the parent's thinking. If parents wish, they are free to live out their lives sacrificing everything for their child. But this will not be in the child's best interest. The same can be said about children. Children, too, can choose to live sacrificing everything for a parent, but this will not truly help the parent.

Even if parent and child are at odds with each other, or if the child comes into this world bearing an incurable illness, mental disorder or physical handicap, parent and child can each do no more than achieve the aims of their own life. Neither can fill the other's shoes and accomplish the other's God-given missions for them.

Whatever kind of past causes might have brought the two of you together in this lifetime, it is important for you to squarely face up to your circumstances, accepting them as they are. If you struggle vehemently against misery or misfortune, it will not bring a true solution. If you can smoothly accept your circumstances, recognizing them as a means of polishing your soul and heightening your spirit, your painful situation will cease to be painful; your tragedies will cease to be tragic.

In terms of outward appearances, it might look as though you are still steeped in misery or distress, just like before. But once your thought has changed, a change in your outward circumstances is sure to follow. You will have graduated from those circumstances, and you can advance to the next step.

Your graduation is for you, yourself. Your 'diploma' can be earned by you alone. For this reason, you yourself must know why it was necessary for you to experience such pain and misery. Once we have each understood this, we can strive forward, supporting and assisting one another so as to graduate as quickly as possible. We have graduated when we have made a change in our thinking.

⤳ It is Natural to Be Happy

Lurking within our minds there are sure to be some discordant, negative thoughts and feelings: strife, anger, jealousy and discontent. All we need to do is make our best effort to shift those thoughts and feelings to the positive side. By 'positive' thinking, I mean harmony, love, affection, mercy, thoughtfulness and appreciation. The unhappiness of each person in this world stems from dark, negative thinking. As soon as you have transformed those dark mental waves to bright ones, the world around you will begin to shine.

This is why I urge you to pour bright thoughts into your subconscious, one after another. Always think of and envision unlimited success, unlimited flourishing, unlimited gratitude and unlimited life. There is just one principle at work: you create the world you live in. The responsibility is yours alone.

There is no reason for you to go on and on suffering. Now, at this moment, let go of your attachments. Let go of your jealousy and your anger. Forgive others, one and all. Do not clutch at the past. It is over and done with.

Yes, without a moment's delay, expel those harsh thoughts

from your mind. Cast your sorrow, your anger and your constricted feelings straight into the divine. Let yourself breathe freely. Stop blaming and judging yourself for what is behind you. A new 'you' has just been born. The 'new you' is facing the future and creating it anew.

You will build a marvellous, resplendent future. Cut through the chains that you have placed around your heart, for they are the source of your anguish. Cast them aside without hesitation. Then pray. Pray for the happiness of mankind.

It does not matter if all sorts of thoughts keep popping into your mind as you pray. Just pray. Pray for peace to prevail on earth. Through your prayer of absolute love, a world of truth will manifest itself around you, and it will be conveyed to the whole of mankind.

You need not suffer any longer.

You need not grieve any longer.

Your prayer has been communicated to heaven.

From the moment when you longed from the bottom of your heart to connect with truth, your world was transformed.

The world of heaven knows your child's unhappiness and pain. Entrust all your anguish to that world – the world of your divinity.

You have suffered and grieved enough. If your child is following a steep path, it is because the child's inner Self has willed it so – so as to reconcile past errors and fulfil the tasks that have been assigned by heaven.

Let your mind be at ease, and know that you, too, must follow your own path to its very end. Do your best to be happy, and free yourself from your pain. You were born in this world to be happy, not to be trapped by anything in the past.

You ought to be happy. It is natural for a human being to be happy.

May Peace Prevail on Earth.

Chapter 2

FACING UP TO
THE EGO

Your life is your own, however you live it. It is you who create your way of living, and it is you who must be satisfied with it. You, and you alone, have the right to make decisions about how to live your life.

How can you make the most of your life? The first step is to return to your starting point. You must discover what it means to be a human being.

Most, however, have not reached this awareness. Of all the people now living in this world, there is virtually no one who fully grasps the truth of their own existence and lives life in real earnest.

When we look around us, we may not see anyone who lives a purely radiant life 100 per cent of the time. We may not see anyone whose life is entirely filled with joy and thankfulness. Somewhere, there is a gloomy shadow hanging over everyone's mind.

Why do people feel so troubled and confused? Why do they behave so badly? Why can't they make up their own minds about how to live their lives? Why do they not live with confidence, their high, spiritual natures shining through for the world to see?

It is because mankind, for the most part, takes so little

interest in the most fundamental questions: what is a human being, and how are we meant to live? If people do not seek the meaning of life, how could they possibly be expected to find it?

Why do people not seek the meaning of life? It is because they do not seek the meaning of death.

A long time ago, human beings forgot who they were and where they came from. They forgot truth – their spirituality. It was then that they began attaching themselves to their material 'self': their physical body. It was then that they created the fear of death.

Because they do not seek the truth of life and death, a great many people are living idle, aimless existences. Not doing what needs to be done, they drift from one day to the next in perpetual apathy. Even in their elder years, many are still worrying and suffering, lost and confused.

⤳ *The Way to a Happy Life*

During the short time that you are to live in this world, what would you most like to know? Do you understand what will become of you after death? Without looking into this question, do you feel that you can live your life with an easy mind?

If you do not know what death is, you might see no choice but to gloomily wait for it with a mixture of uneasiness, fear and attachment to this world. With death only a short distance away, are you going to let this lifetime come to an end without preparing for it at all? Can you be satisfied that way?

If you do not know even a little about what death is, it means that you have been letting your life slip away from you. You have spent a lot of time complicating your life with various struggles, never allowing time for the vital question of how you should be living it.

Death seems altogether fearsome to you. Deep down, your heart is filled with cowardice and uncertainty. With this state of mind, you are likely either to fall apart or else try to run away each time something unexpected confronts you.

Because you lack true confidence in your life, your thoughts have been mostly preoccupied with your dependence on others and your attachment to material things. Your attachments have turned into an insatiable craving to possess. Attitudes like these have pervaded your heart and made it their prisoner.

Surely you know that when you go to 'the world after death', none of what you have been attached to can be taken with you. Yet have you really and truly faced up to this fact? The process of dying is the process of letting go of the ego and everything that the ego clings to. If we can go through this process, we have discovered the way to a happy life.

✐ What Can You Take With You?

During this lifetime, you may have attained a certain position. You may have acquired wealth, property, a home and so forth. Eventually, though, you must leave all of it behind and start a new journey on your own, parting even from the family and friends that you love.

Yet when you go to the world after death, there *are* things that you can take with you. You can take everything that belongs to the spirit. You can take the fruits of your good thoughts and actions: love, sincerity, goodness and beauty.

What this means is that death is not really separate from life. The way to die is the way to live. The way to live is the way to die. Life and death are not opposites: death is an extension of life.

Until now, most of humanity has viewed the meaning of life entirely in material terms. Because people place first importance on material things, science has developed and material civilization has flourished. Yet in order to attain material benefits, how much strife have we gone through? How much blood have we shed? The history of material culture has also been the history of struggle and destruction.

At the individual level, too, people have had to be

constantly at work struggling against others and kicking them down. They have spared no effort, however ignoble, in profiting themselves and satisfying their own cravings.

Sooner or later, by enduring, persevering, agonizing and struggling, people somehow attain their material goals. Yet in the end, death will not allow them to bring those attainments along with them. Why, then, do people toil and labour so hard to acquire those things? It is because they believe that the very purpose of life is to keep on fighting and struggling – even though all that they accumulate will eventually have to be discarded.

The Ultimate Attachment: The Ego

Mankind's present way of living could be described as a series of attachments. People attach themselves to their dearly loved husband, wife or children; they attach themselves to their house or their land, their position or their authority; they attach themselves to their store of knowledge, their religion, their nation or ethnic group. For most people, to live means to be attached to something.

When all is said and done, our ultimate attachment is our attachment to the ego. It is our attachment to our own life. It all started when we forgot where life came from, and began to think that it was something that could be lost. When this thought took shape, we felt helpless and afraid. We searched through our material surroundings for something to hang on to. We sought a way to assign value and meaning to our lives. And so we created a new 'self' and a new world: the world of the ego.

What is the ego? The ego is energy. It is none other than the accumulated energy of our own way of thinking, our own emotions, our own experiences, our own beliefs. Each of us has created an ego, and it is no exaggeration to say that this ego is what maintains and perpetuates our own way of living.

Do you truly know yourself? Before you can answer this, you

must accurately recognize the nature of your ego – the thoughts and emotions that are at work within you. You must also correctly assess your responses to those thoughts and emotions.

At the bottom of every heart, there flows a stream of desires. People long to make themselves into a certain something, and they make fruitless efforts toward achieving those desires while clinging tightly to their consciousness of self. This consciousness of self is, itself, the basis of the ego.

The ego is the composite of all thoughts and attitudes such as competitiveness, the desire to possess something or become something. When we come face to face with our ego, we are shocked to discover how self-centered and desirous our daily thoughts are – how spiteful, sly and calculating our thoughts can be.

Each time a new issue arises in our life, we form an impression based upon our previous feelings and experiences, held within the ego. Through those impressions, we respond to each new issue with a new thought or action. In this way, our previous feelings and experiences keep reinforcing themselves, urging us into more desires and ambitions.

To realize their desires and ambitions, people will endure insult and humiliation. They experience deep sadness, fierce anger, violent jealousy, strong competitiveness, insufferable resentment and discontent. Sometimes they lose their sense of personal worth entirely. These kinds of experiences can drive people into even deeper attachments. For example, if someone feels bitterly humiliated by poverty, the desire for wealth and authority can become abnormally strong. One dark and sorrowful experience can act as a foothold from which we leap into even more intense desires.

All these emotions and experiences are the work of the ego, nothing else. To satisfy the ego, people strongly feel that they must become something or own something. This is why they keep making vain efforts, piteous and corrupt efforts, over and over again.

⌐ *The Cause of Fear and Pain*

Making whatever efforts they possibly can, people achieve what they have been striving for and become what they wanted to become. Then, they start to feel fearful of losing what they have obtained or what they have become. They fear losing their position, their reputation, their talent, their knowledge, their family, wealth, popularity, authority, and all that they have accumulated. This fear is very deeply rooted. The loss of those things would seem unbearably painful.

In reality, our true Self desires nothing, because it already possesses everything. But human beings have lost all memory of this. And so they cling to the ego, longing to confirm their sense of worth and self-importance.

To satisfy the ego, human beings will endure no end of bitterness. However much humiliation and insult they have to suffer, the power to endure it will be provided to them. The ego has this kind of fierce vigour and determination.

But when your ego is wounded, or you are forced to swallow your ego, you sustain a violent shock. Sometimes you cannot call forth the power to bear even the slightest difficulty. This goes to show how the ego has come to function as the basic motive power that keeps people going. Meanwhile, because human beings have this ego, they are followed about by pain and frustration, disappointment and misery.

To avoid injury to their ego people unconsciously devise ways of protecting themselves. Yet what happens is that these self-protective efforts always end up producing more fears.

Why do they produce more fears? After using all possible means to establish things that will satisfy your ego, you focus on preserving what you have attained, thinking: *I must not lose this. I must not lose my health. I must not lose my happiness. I must not lose my sleep. I must not lose my life.* No sooner do you think these things than fear springs up in your heart, turning into pains and agonies that assail you. You then try to insulate yourself against your pain with more defensive measures and attitudes.

Thus, the unconscious actions that you take in order to escape from your pain continue to generate new fears and agonies. Because there is the ego, fear is born. Because there is fear, pain is born. Because there is pain, the ego is hurt; and so it goes, on and on. These self-created thought vibrations, recorded in the subconscious, keep spinning round and round along with other thoughts like them. They spin endlessly, with intense vigour, never resolving themselves.

Assess Yourself Accurately

Your *ego* is not *you.* Your ego is something you created. Once you understand what the ego is, it will be possible for you to discover your true Self. Knowing your true Self is the most important thing you can do. It was because you did not know your true Self that you got on the wrong track in life.

Before thinking that you want to become this or that, before feeling that you want to be sure of this or that, before you overestimate yourself, before you blame yourself, the first thing you must do is to make the right assessment of yourself.

Where did you come from? What is your purpose in this world? Consider your present surroundings, your educational background, your outlook on life, your religion, your country, your parents, friends, brothers and sisters, the way you grew up, your personality, your future, and so on. In order to know yourself, you need to reflect upon your attitudes and experiences in this way. You need to thoroughly study yourself to get a full and clear perspective on what your thinking consists of and how it functions.

Before trying to become a particular kind of person or obtain a certain thing, it is important for you to know yourself. Without knowing anything about your true Self, if you just impulsively try to do this or that, or to obtain this or that, however you may race and struggle your efforts will be futile.

By closely observing your thoughts, your emotions, your actions and your reactions to things, it will be possible for you to distinguish your ego from your true Self. On the other hand, if you are totally unaware of who and what you really are, it will be very difficult for you to attain what you strive for or to become what you want to become.

When you know yourself in depth, the truth will come into view for the first time. Once you recognize your inadequate 'self', your incomplete 'self', your greedy 'self', your ignorant 'self', your petty 'self', your fragile 'self', your arrogant 'self', and your failed 'self' – and identify all those 'selves' as being unreal – you will arrive at the starting point of your life.

For anyone, looking closely at yourself and knowing yourself has an element of discomfort and fear to it. This is because no one wants to face their own secrets. Yet the point is, if you keep avoiding these things out of fear, you will spend your whole life being unable to walk along your own true path.

 Mankind Must Change its Direction

You are not the only one who is selfish. You are not the only one who is weak. You are not the only one who is cowardly, soiled, unsightly or inferior. You are not the only one who has lied. You are not the only one who is pretending or has shameful secrets. Ninety-nine per cent of mankind is just like you. No, I should say 99.99 per cent *plus*. You do not need to be so intensely afraid. You are not so exceptionally bad. All of mankind carries the same burdens as you do.

This is why mankind's suffering, unhappiness and turmoil have not come to an end: people who have shirked the task of knowing themselves have had to keep suffering all their lives. On the other hand, those who have come to know themselves have been able to take their first step forward. When we reach this point, we can begin to clear up questions like *What kind of existence am I? Why are we here on this planet earth?*

Mankind as a whole has been on the wrong track. Instead of recognizing their wondrous qualities, people have been looking only at their weak points, blaming and judging themselves all the time. Since ages past, they have been treating themselves and others as though human beings were fundamentally sinful, mortal existences. This is how they have been taught and guided. They have always been focusing on their own disharmony, their own imperfection, their own vice. Since they were born, they have lived with the feeling that their imperfect, ailing, sinful selves are their true, original selves. They have seen no alternative but to recognize those negative qualities and believe in them.

As people have persistently thought of themselves as no good, unclean and unsightly, by the strength of their convictions, their self-negating thoughts have further enlarged and intensified. As a result, their lives have unfolded in misfortune and failure, just as they expected.

It is a natural law that people's lives unfold according to their thoughts and beliefs. This is why unhappy things, ugly things, inharmonious and imperfect things keep happening one after another. Because the whole of mankind keeps adding power and conviction to negative elements, the tragedies of struggle, agony, disaster and sorrow have not come to an end.

If mankind keeps moving in this direction, there will be no way for those tragedies to go away. On the contrary, by adding power to its increasingly negative beliefs, mankind is rushing full speed ahead along the road to destruction. Somewhere along the way, we must put a stop to it. We must change our direction.

✑ *Discover* the Real You

To reverse this direction, each member of mankind has to wake up and see that their inadequate, miserable self is not their true Self. All these things are nothing more than the vanishing traces of mistaken beliefs and actions carried over from the past. In his classic work *God and Man*, Masahisa Goi explains it this way:

> A human being is originally a spirit from God, and not a karmic[2] or sinful existence. We live under the constant guidance and protection of guardian spirits and divinities.
>
> All the sufferings of this world occur when human beings' mistaken thoughts, conceived during past existences and continuing until the present, manifest themselves at the time of their vanishing away.
>
> Any affliction, once it has taken shape in this phenomenal world, is destined to vanish into nothingness. Therefore, you must firmly believe that your suffering is fading away, and that from now on your life will be happier. Even in any difficulty, forgive yourself and forgive others, love yourself and love others. If you continually perform actions of love, sincerity and forgiveness, while always thanking your divine and spiritual protectors and praying for the peace of the world, you as an individual, as well as mankind, will be able to realize true spiritual awakening.
>
> This is what I think and put into practice.[3]

When we have deeply understood the meaning of these words, we can genuinely know ourselves for the first time. When we put this understanding into practice, we can take an entirely new approach to life.

As you keep seeking it, you will gradually come to recognize your own true identity. Step by step you will become aware that your former 'self', created in the world of your ego, was not your true Self. You will know that the deficient 'you' that blamed and judged yourself, the 'you' that thought you were a fool, that could not love or forgive yourself, is not the *real you*. Instead of being obsessed with the faults and weaknesses of your present personality, you will come to discover

your luminous inner Self and the limitless capabilities that
you hold within you.

Focus on the Infinite

When you truly know yourself, there will be nothing at all
to bind or restrict your heart. You will freely command the
infinite energy, wisdom and power that are flowing abundantly
to you. Nothing will be lacking. Nothing will be wasted. Everything will be in perfect harmony. You will hardly remember the
pain and the misery of the past.

Do not let your heart be a prisoner of the past. Never pull
the past back toward you or torment yourself over it. The past
is gone. However you might regret the past and however you
might repent over it, it is behind you. However irreparable the
damage might seem to be, it is over and done with. Do not look
back. Instead, look to the future. Look to the clear light of
truth. When you do this, your sadness and anguish will instantly disappear.

As images from the past keep emerging and vanishing
away, your true Self can gradually come shining through. All
you have to do is to thoroughly and steadily keep turning your
thoughts toward the light.

Never hold on to bad thoughts. Never express bad
thoughts in word or in action. Focus only on the infinite:
infinite love, infinite life, infinite health, infinite flourishing,
infinite betterment. This is the way for mankind to turn toward a bright and peaceful future.

As each of us lives this way, calling forth the marvellous
capabilities that are inherent within us, we can each do our part
in building a brilliant new, spiritual culture on the planet earth.

May Peace Prevail on Earth.

❈

Chapter 3

DEVELOP YOUR INTUITION

In my native language, Japanese, we write the word for intuition in three characters. The first character (直) means *direct*. The second character (観) means *perception*. The third character (力) means *power*. By looking at these written characters, we can understand that *intuition* is the faculty or power to perceive something directly.

Here is how I would explain it. The word 'intuition' refers to the functioning of an unseen power originating at the source of our life. It is the power that allows our mind to respond directly to God, the Law of the Universe.

To live vibrantly and energetically, and to accomplish our true purpose in life, we must develop our intuition and make full use of it. Intuition is, indeed, the most important thing in life.

This power called intuition is something that everyone has been endowed with, from the very beginning. We have each been provided with the ability to intently perceive the intention of the Universal Law – the vibrations emanating from heaven. People with highly developed intuition never experience misery or discord in their lives, because they are living and expressing the will of the Universe itself.

The Universe is continually radiating its precepts to anyone and everyone on an equal basis. Those who can directly tune in to it and naturally accept it, just as it is, are those who can live in a world of perfect harmony, free from suffering and misfortune. They, in turn, radiate happiness outward to others. All of us possess the power of intuition. What ultimately decides our fate is whether or not we can make full use of it.

There are many people in this world who end their lives without using their intuitive faculties even once. There are many who depend only on practical knowledge and on the information gathered during their current lifetime. It is no exaggeration to say that those people are the unhappy ones, the ones who are suffering.

We need to realize that there is something beyond the scope of commonly accepted attitudes and conventional knowledge – a strong, invisible power that works on our lives. No matter how much effort and patience we may be exerting to expand our knowledge and demonstrate it to others, this alone cannot bring us fulfilment.

Actually, there are people who lead worthy lives relying on neither practical nor factual knowledge. These people are fully aware of the wonders of intuition, and they understand it. As they rely entirely on their intuition, they are never led astray by outside influences. They have a strong will to follow their conscience, and they live with confidence.

On the other hand, there are also people who only follow what others say, swallowing it whole. They imitate others at all times, without ever exercising their own judgment or setting their own guidelines. These people have not yet recognized and developed their intuitive faculties.

Developing your intuition means cultivating your faculty for allowing the vibrations from heaven to be received directly into your body. Once this power is developed, you can pursue your true way of life without imitating others. This is something you must do, for your way of life is different from anyone else's, and it can be accomplished by no one other than yourself.

Once we have developed our intuition, we shall never fall into misfortune. We will never attract suffering and tragedy, nor will we become entangled in discord. Since our actions will originate in the Great Harmony of the Universe, we will be able to emanate unending happiness and prosperity into this world.

It is because people's intuition is dim or inactive, or because they are unaware of their intuition, that they have diverted from their true path in life. They have placed themselves in a state of delusion and suffering, experiencing the same needless miseries over and over again. If only they were to open their eyes to their inner, intuitive power, their view on life would change completely. They would clearly discern their own path, as if the blindfolds had been lifted from their eyes.

Since intuition is the faculty for directly receiving the vibrations of the Universal Law, when this power is inhibited, people are unable to perceive those fine vibrations accurately. As a result, they easily stray in the wrong direction, and encounter misfortune, suffering and miseries that might have been avoided.

When our intuition is highly developed, the intention of the Universe is directly felt in our hearts, clearly indicating how we should proceed. If we are constantly attuned to this divine vibration, we can spontaneously give expression to it in the natural course of our lives.

The 'Universe' could also be called Infinite Life, Infinite Creativity or God. All the faculties of this Infinite Life can be directly conveyed into our minds. Unlimited capability, unending happiness, true freedom, a calming sense of beauty, boundless vitality – all these qualities can be directly conveyed to us. When we exhibit these qualities, everything flourishes and we experience true fulfilment.

Why do we not reach out to catch the limitless qualities being radiated to us? Why do we not even try to receive them?

If each member of humanity were to awaken to their intuition, I feel that the world would immediately be led to peace.

But the awakening of individuals is a difficult goal to achieve. Why is this so? It is because most people are entirely preoccupied with fulfilling their immediate, short-term desires. Even though the precepts of the Universal Law are resonating everywhere, how many people respond to this fine resonance? Very, very few. Only those who have acknowledged their original identity can respond to it. As for the others, no matter how the Universal Law acts upon them, they take no notice. Driven by the impetus of their erroneous thinking, they chase round and round, pursued by their own miseries.

Loss of Intuition

Look closely at the lifestyles of those who have lost their intuition. As if caught in a web, they are entrapped by their materially-oriented desires. Believing that happiness comes solely from the attainment of material goals, they live their lives without utilizing their intuition.

Even though they may already possess material wealth, they are bent on acquiring more. They have become enslaved by their possessions. They are tossed about and controlled by their attachment to wealth.

Think about the plight of the highly educated. In spite of the public acclaim they receive, many of them are caged within the boundaries of their own knowledge and have lost their intuition.

Think about those who believe themselves to be devout, but are suffering because their lives are restricted by formalism, dogma and convention. Since they have lost their intuition, they are unable to live in peace.

All these people have inadvertently built walls in front of themselves, motivated by their short-sighted purposes and desires. Those very walls are what stop them from moving ahead. People are now either treating those rigid, thick,

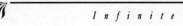

self-created walls as if they were enemies to be struggled against, or else they are trying to run away from them.

People who have lost their intuition lack true understanding. They believe whatever is generally believed by the majority, and have built their lives around those beliefs. Having lost track of their inner power and purpose in this world, they are quite at sea, not knowing what they should do. Not one of them has a sense of true fulfilment. Not one of them is happy. Not one of them is calling forth their true, God-given power.

The majority of today's people are living this way. In living without their intuition, they have created a world of illusion, the world of the ego.

⤳ *Accept Nothing in This World of Illusion*

Never accept anything in this world of illusion. Until your intuition is enhanced, until you have broken down all the obstacles built by yourself, until you have rejected and given up every belief accumulated through the functioning of your ego, do not accept a thing. Until you call forth your own distinct intuition, you will not be able to discover your new, clear purpose in life. And unless your intuitive power reverberates straight through from the bottom of your soul, it is not real.

Whether it be authority, fame, honour, wealth, money, property, family name, knowledge, education, death, illness, trouble, misery, crime, sin or desire, never trust in anything, not even yourself – not until you have fully grasped the truth of your existence.

People are being crushed under the weight of all that they have taken in, yet they are still demanding more. But if we believed in all the knowledge, information and know-how that inundate our world today, we could easily stray in the wrong direction.

Whether or not you believe something should be determined only by your own authentic intuition. True intuition, and true intuition alone, can show you what to accept and what to reject. Even though other people may believe something, that in itself does not mean that you must also believe it. Your true and unerring intuition should be the decision-maker for each and every moment in your life.

Human beings are originally divinity itself – infinite life itself. They are not the conglomerations of avarice, greed or ego that they appear to be. The problem arises when people do not recognize their true, fundamental nature. This causes them to either put on airs or underestimate themselves. After all, how can you possibly stay on the right track unless you have at least a faint sense of the superb intuitive power, talent and vocational calling that exist within you?

So that everyone can discover these qualities within themselves, we must avoid forcing our ideas and opinions on others. We must try not to intrude into other people's freedom or beliefs: this is a fundamental principle. Even between parent and child, it is important to respect one another's individuality and keep interference to a minimum.

In reality, though, this is quite difficult. Until now, we have always listened to the learned, to those who are called leaders, experts or knowledgeable people. We have accepted their words as being unquestionably true. Indeed, some of what they have said may have been true, but often enough, their ideas exist on a plane with similar ideas, generated by people who vie with each other for dominance or authority.

It is neither your duty nor your destiny to be moulded by other people's ideas. If you have been living this way, it is the result of your lack of intuition. You are the one responsible for finding your way in life – only then can you be absolutely confident, with no doubts and no regrets. Only then can you experience the true joy of living.

⌒ *Recognize Your Intuitive Power*

It is time for you to recognize your true intuitive power, and acquire the courage to reject everything else. To unquestioningly assimilate the deluge of information that engulfs this world could result in great confusion. With careful consideration, you must firmly reject what needs to be rejected. In many cases, people are burdened with misfortunes and sufferings that are quite uncalled for, just because they could not say 'no' or reject something when they had to.

In the end, those misfortunes and sufferings were un-preventable, since they resulted from people's own decisions, made under the assumption that they would turn out satis-factorily. But in order to prevent those same kinds of mistakes from recurring in the future, I urge you to live your life in a way that lets you become conscious of your intuition as soon as possible.

> *Intuition always exists in you.*
> *It was there from the beginning.*
> *It is not man-made, nor does it need to be.*
> *It is within you.*
> *It is around you.*
> *It is you.*
>
> *There is no need to search for it.*
> *You simply need to become aware of it.*
> *Become aware that you are a spirit from God.*
>
> *You are no longer asleep.*
> *You are no longer dreaming.*
> *You have come to see the truth.*
>
> *The truth is*
> *That you are a child of God,*
> *Shining brightly.*

Truth is the activity of an awakened consciousness. It is the consciousness of divinity, conveyed to us through intuition.

Until today you may have left your intuition untouched,

leaving it for another day. But it exists now, at this very moment. Intuition is not of the future, nor is it of the past: it is of the here and now. Truth and intuition exist at all times in every human being.

It is not your struggle for freedom that will set you free – it is the truth that will set you free. It is your intuition that will set you free. You must take hold of the chance to discover your true Self, the real you. You must let your present self merge with your true, original Self.

Our true Self is not motivated by other people's thoughts or expectations. We must receive our motivation from the intuitive wisdom of the Universe that naturally exists within us.

ᔑ *Do Not Look at a Fragmented Picture*

When our actions are guided by our intuition, there is no emotional complication, no conflict or tension. Even though, from other people's point of view, it might seem as though we are putting forth a lot of effort, we, ourselves, experience no exertion and no strain. Our whole existence, being truly awakened, is living with joy.

On the other hand, when we try to reason things out without having a full perspective, we are only seeing a fragmented picture. This often plants seeds of conflict in the mind. Unless our thoughts rise from the very source of our mind, through intuition, we will not be able to find true solutions.

For example, think about those who have awakened to the degree that they feel pangs of conscience over their desire for material possessions. They now feel a disgust for material things, and try to be completely free from avarice. But the more they struggle to be free, the more preoccupied they become. Instead of truly becoming free, they become obsessed by the idea of becoming free from avarice. Their obsession inhibits their spontaneity. They are distancing themselves from true freedom.

The same might be said of health-conscious people. The

harder they try to be healthy, the more difficult it becomes for them to run away from their anxiety over illness.

Rather than letting go of their fixed ideas and whole-heartedly praying to their infinite, divine Selves, people have been attaching themselves to ideas that come from the limited scope of their superficial knowledge. If you keep looking at a fragmented picture, your attempts at problem-solving cannot bring a fundamental solution. They only produce more conflict, confusion, misery and fear.

If those who are fearful were only aware of their intuitive power, they would strive to identify the source of their fear. They would look straight into their fear to determine what it consisted of without averting their eyes or trying to run away from it. In examining their fear, they would find that it had ceased of its own accord.

To do this is neither courageous nor cowardly; it simply entails examining your fear and understanding it, through intuition, so that you no longer have any fear to run away from. Your fear has been extinguished.

Whatever kind of anguish it might be, if you try to run away from it, you will never really be able to dispel it. The solution to a problem is found in looking straight into the cause, even though it may be secret or shameful. Look at the source of your problem, without averting your eyes, and you will find the key to its solution.

⌒ *Attune Your Mind to Your True Self*

How wonderful it will be when we are completely free from desire and greed. All our suffering, sadness and fear are born from desire and greed. When people free themselves from all the desire and greed that are concealed within them, they will experience happiness far greater than they ever imagined possible.

People today have become obsessed with various demands and desires. They have come to believe that possession, whether material or intellectual, is the one and only thing in life. Their minds are fully occupied by the pleasure and sense of superiority derived from possessing all sorts of material and intellectual assets. Instead of wishing to heighten their character or give expression to their true identity, they aim only at obtaining something from the outside world or at becoming something in terms of the outside world.

The human subconscious is filled with aspirations of becoming a person of consequence, of having a good name, of having a title or authority. We have become enslaved by these ideas, which have been drilled into our subconscious over a long period of time. We have been instilling these values in our minds, over and over again. This vicious circle has brought this planet, and the human race, to the brink of collapse.

At this point, someone has to put an end to this historical vicious circle. It will take considerable courage to achieve this. It will mean walking away from our half-hearted, lackadaisical attitudes. It will mean freeing ourselves from long-established habits; but, in severing our inclination to strive for possessions or status, we will be reborn to a new way of life.

⤳ God's Mind is Our Mind

To discover this new way of life, we must cultivate the intuitive power that we were born with. We must switch over to an intuitively-guided lifestyle. Using our intuition, we can achieve an unerring, brilliant life.

We human beings are originally motivated to live just as our intuition tells us to live. At all times, human beings exist within the omnipotence of the Universe, or 'God'.

Though we have come to look upon God as an outside existence, separate from ourselves, in reality, nothing separates us from God. There is no distance between God and ourselves, nor is there any interval when we live apart from God.

Because we live in God, God's mind is our mind. When we talk about our 'true Self' we are talking about God. By attuning our mind to our true Self, we can directly understand the divine intention: this is what intuition is.

The notion of a distance between God and man, or the idea that God and man are separate existences, is false, and comes from having forgotten truth. In reality, we are firmly and fully united with God through an infallible spiritual bond.

As God communicates with us, God's intention spontaneously reverberates within us by way of intuition. If we always think of God, pray to God and attune our consciousness to God, God's intention will be projected into this world through our minds. People whose intuitive faculties function naturally and smoothly are living their lives according to the design of God.

Intuition is a power discerned only by those who believe in God's love. It is an absolute power, indispensable to our life in this world.

⮫ *True Intuition or Subconscious Influences?*

Even if desires are now churning in your heart, intuition can nonetheless be received, without fail, at the moment when you attune your mind to your true Self: God. Intuition is not a special power exclusive to the honourable, the pure, the noble or the virtuous. Intuition is a universal power provided to us all.

Since the power of intuition transcends everything, it has nothing to do with age, sex, race, culture or academic background. Though you might be a criminal, or have a sinful, sordid or disgraceful heart, intuition can be attained at the moment when you direct your mind to your true Self.

The essential condition for developing your intuitive power is to always have your mind attuned to your true Self. You must also be aware that, if thoughts and ideas flash into your mind or flicker through your thoughts when you are not attuned to your true Self, those thoughts and ideas do not come from your true Self.

When our minds are not attuned to our true Self, we could hardly expect the vibrations of truth to come resonating through. Therefore, if various thoughts and ideas come to us in a flash, when our minds are not attuned to our true Self, those thoughts and ideas are not the product of true intuition, but come from subconscious influences. A distinction must be made between the two.

As our egocentric desires keep repeating themselves in our minds, they sometimes take the form of flashing ideas that recur during a moment of forgetfulness. It is important to recognize that these phenomena are not examples of true intuition. True intuition and subconscious phenomena have entirely different functions.

Intuitive power is constantly flowing into people like you, who cherish a strong desire for world peace, because world peace in itself is the desire of your true Self. When you are faced with a decision, direct your mind to your true Self and pray for world peace. The wavelength of your prayer will synchronize with the wavelength of your true, divine Self, and it will be conveyed to you in the form of intuition. Your intuition will naturally come through to you, sharp and clear, when you pray for the peace of mankind.

As we continue to develop and refine our intuition, the day will certainly come when our highest hopes will come to fruition.

May Peace Prevail on Earth.

Chapter 4

ENERGY AND
POWER

Many people wonder *Why do I have this empty feeling? Why do I feel that something is missing?*

Human beings experience a wide range of feelings and emotions. Sometimes we experience an unproductive, empty feeling, or a feeling of loneliness or isolation. Sometimes we experience bright feelings of joy and exhilaration.

Why is it that feelings of emptiness, sadness and loneliness arise in people's hearts? Those feelings occur when people blame and torment themselves for letting the days go by without working or accomplishing anything. People naturally tend to worry and accuse themselves when they let the days slip by in idleness, not achieving anything. Because they have not utilized and released the energy within them, it remains pent up in their bodies.

Human beings are given infinite abilities, coming from God. These abilities are meant to be utilized. In using our abilities, we produce effects on other people and on our surroundings. This is our fundamental reason for living. This is why God provides us with an unlimited source of energy.

Our God-given energy must be processed through our physical body in order to be sent outward. As much as we can, we have to give out our energy, exerting a positive influence on the people around us, on our society and on our country. It is our fundamental nature to do this.

When you feel that you have striven and have done the best you can for yourself, you can, indeed, have a certain sense of fulfilment. Yet as you become more and more awakened to your spirituality, you will not get a sense of fulfilment from using your energy only for your own benefit. Even if you achieve success in your own work, it will seem as though something is lacking.

As you work hard day after day and make efforts on your own behalf, you might become wealthy. Your family might feel happy. You might make gains in terms of position, reputation or authority. In using your energy for these things, you might feel a sense of contentment, but at the bottom of your heart, you will not be completely satisfied.

Why will you not be satisfied? It is because the energy that is provided to you is meant to be burned for the sake of humanity, according to the design of heaven. It is not meant to be used only for yourself. If mankind as a whole is enriched, if you render service to society through your work, or if many people become happy because of your work, you will never be distracted by feelings of sadness, loneliness or emptiness.

If you spend the day in apathy, without making any effort, not even on your own behalf, you are likely to suffer pangs of conscience. You will say to yourself *I didn't do a thing all day except eat. I am disgusted with myself. What a lazy good-for-nothing I am! What am I really living for?*

ᔆ *Clear the Way for New Energy*

Do not let yourself fall into the habit of wasting your days, one after the other. Even if yesterday was spent in idleness, or even if it was a miserable day for you, filled with failure, illness or accidents, once you retired for the night it was all behind you. When you woke up this morning, it was time to greet a brand new day.

Today's new morning is not a continuation of yesterday. With each new morning, our lives are revitalized. We are provided with new energy from God to replace the energy that was used yesterday.

However, if we do not use up the energy that has been given to us in a day, the unused portion will stay with us. Just like a fire that has not reached complete combustion, our leftover, imperfectly burned energy will continue to smoulder within us.

We must never allow our surplus energy to smoulder within us. The way to burn all of it is to continually direct our energy toward others, toward the outside world. As much as possible, we must keep giving of our energy to society and to our country. This is why new life, brimming over with energy, has been provided to us today.

If we have done nothing all day, it means that our energy has not gone anywhere. Our energy is abundantly overflowing. We must use it, all of it, before the day is over.

Why must we use all of it up today? It is because new energy will again be provided to us tomorrow. I think you are familiar with the biblical phrase: *No man putteth new wine into old wineskins.*[4] If there is still old wine remaining in a wineskin, new wine (new energy, abounding with wisdom) will be mixed with the old. The new is easily spoiled by the old. As long as there is old wine left in the wineskin, all the wine will turn stale and unpalatable. Unless the old wine has entirely disappeared, the true aroma and flavour of the new wine will not greet our senses.

The same can be said about energy. Inevitably, the new will mix with the old. What is new and fresh will be altered by what is old and stale. This is why we must do our utmost to send out every bit of today's energy today.

✎ Use All Your Energy Today

When you wake up in the morning, do you feel as though you cannot bring yourself to do anything at all? Do you feel too sluggish to start your work? Do you feel as though today will be just one more meaningless day? If so, it is because the residue of yesterday's energy is still pent up within you. What I would suggest is that you devise some means of burning up that stagnant energy. You could get some exercise, try singing a song, or go jogging, and so on. You must clear the way for today's new energy to come through to you. Unless you learn how to do this, you will have to carry the old, pent-up energy with you. Then, through the functioning of that old, stale energy, today's new, God-given energy will be sullied, and you will find yourself whiling away the day without achieving anything.

This is why I urge you to fully utilize the energy that is provided to you in the course of the day. If you think *I'll save my energy for tomorrow or for the next day*, you will not be able to make the most of your life.

There are many people who want to go a little further, but stop themselves with the thought: *If I take another step, I won't be able to do a thing tomorrow*, or *If I keep on working, I might get sick*. Their true feeling is that they would like to get some more work done. They would like to burn more of their energy. They would like to offer more to humanity. They would like to study more or keep bettering themselves. But another part of them is saying: *If you do, you will be tired tomorrow. You need your sleep. You'll get sick. You'd better stop now.*

When you are in this situation, it is not necessary for you to put a damper on your true feelings. If you feel the desire to do more, it is because you still have more energy. Because you have a surplus of energy, you feel that you would like to work, you would like to study, you would like to finish what you have been doing.

If you had really used up all your energy, you would not get the feeling that you wanted to do more. If you tried to do more, you would be unable to. You would only feel like sleeping. This would mean that you had used up the energy given to you for the day; and so you would sleep. And when you awoke the next morning, new energy would again be supplied to you without limitation.

There is no necessity for you to deliberately hold yourself in check with your own self-created form of common sense, stopping yourself from doing what you want to do. When you deliberately inhibit the use of your energy, the inhibited portion stays pent up within you. It is then converted into a form of energy spent on blaming and judging yourself, regretting the things you wanted to do and grieving over the things you could not do.

Watch How You Use Your Energy

Our energy does not come to us in varying forms. We do not receive one kind of energy for work, another kind for gladness, another for recreation and another for healing our illness. We are given a certain amount of energy. The way we live our life is, in other words, the way we use all the energy provided to us.

The energy we receive is without form or hue. With our own free will we each decide how to use our given energy through our physical bodies. If we do not expend the very last bit of pent-up energy, we will be unable to sleep soundly. In order to get a good night's sleep, we have to fully use all the energy provided to us for that one day.

Let us say that you have spent the whole day in lethargy, without getting anything done. Now, your unused energy is stagnating inside you. Where will this unused energy be directed? There is a danger that your leftover energy might be used for accusing and hurting yourself. There is a mechanism in the human psychology that aims at expending the full amount of energy remaining in the body, in one way or another, so that it will not be carried over to the next day. And, oddly enough, people are in the habit of expending that spare energy for detrimental purposes. Consequently, they end up directing their leftover energy into thoughts like *I am lazy, I am contempt-ible, I am a no-good, miserable person.*

It is not good to inhibit the proper use of your energy by making judgments against yourself. Instead, try to utilize more and more of your energy for good purposes, for the benefit of mankind as a whole.

Throughout the day, until you go to bed at night, you might be praying for peace to prevail on earth. You might be converting your energy to bright thoughts of infinite love, life and joy. If you are doing this, it means that, right up to the end, the energy given to you today is being expended for the sake of many people. Your way of using your energy is having a good effect on society and mankind. Because of this, you sleep well at night, and awaken the next morning with a refreshed feeling. New energy is provided to you from heaven, and you again distribute that new energy for the sake of mankind, directing your mind toward constructive goals.

Energy used for the peace of mankind functions in unison with God. Energy used for immersing your thoughts in bright light is perfectly harmonized with God. God's energy, itself, is perfectly clear and transparent, reflecting infinite love, joy and light itself. When you pray for the peace of mankind, you are emitting God's infinite energy outwards through mind and body. This is why you never have an empty feeling growing within you.

Why do you not experience feelings of emptiness, loneli-ness or anguish? Even if a portion of the day's energy should pass through your mind in the form of anguish or pain, in the end you will not blame yourself or harbour any regrets. If you conclude the day by expending your last bit of energy on bright thoughts and prayers, there is no need for your anguish to be perpetuated.

◌ *Wielding the Energy of Nations*

At any and all times, we can resolutely use our energy in

any way we choose to. We are free to use our energy for bad purposes if that is our desire. We can use it for the ruin of an opponent, or for driving someone into illness if it is our will to do so.

Why is it that mankind's energy has been directed toward war? It is because each individual has been using their energy for unconstructive purposes. As each citizen of a nation keeps misusing his or her own energy, the accumulation of this misdirected energy continues to expand rapidly until it finally erupts in the form of conflict with other nations.

When war breaks out among nations, what should be done to enable those countries to find peace? The best thing would be for all citizens of those countries to use their energy for wonderful, harmonious purposes. The people who make up the nation need to utilize their energy in a way that will lead to their spiritual awakening.

The question of whether a nation achieves peace and harmony depends on the way each person who sustains the nation uses his or her God-given energy. It depends on whether this energy is directed toward constructive or destructive goals. In the long run, what leads a country either to peace or to downfall is the daily thinking of each one of its people.

Individuals and nations who drive themselves to war, are, in the final analysis, using their wondrous, God-given energy to generate strife, hatred and jealousy, and to sharpen their own appetite for monopoly.

Illness is another way in which pent-up energy manifests itself. If we do not properly use up all our energy, it continues to accumulate, and eventually pollutes the physical body in the form of illness. If we emit all our excess energy for the benefit of the world, through peace prayers or else by steadfastly focusing on the infiniteness within us, our illnesses can ultimately be healed.

People who pray for the happiness of mankind and know the importance of converting their thoughts to bright ones always emit their energy in like manner with the activity of God itself. If we are doing the very same work as God is doing, we could hardly expect to be unhappy, could we?

⟨ *Energy is Power*

Energy is power. Yet instead of drawing out and developing our own wondrous power, most of us are giving our power away. We are handing it over to things in the outside world. At the same time, we are suffering from the very power that we ourselves have given away.

Originally, the outside world has no power to control us. People may think that there is power outside themselves, and it may appear to be that way, but in reality the outside world has no power of its own at all.

True, original power is always within us. It is power from God. There is no other power than this. If we let our own will coincide with the limitless power and intelligence of God, overflowing with splendour and dignity, we can give expression to that marvellous power through our existence.

Far from manifesting the power of their divinity, most people are subordinating themselves to external things. Meanwhile, all true power, every bit of it, remains entirely within themselves. If it looks as though there is power outside their true Self, that power is an illusion. We must wake up to the fact that the wisdom of our divine Self holds the power to unlock the future. We must not let ourselves be controlled by anything else.

Many people think that it is the fault of some other person – or of some circumstance or event – that they are feeling such anguish. In thinking that way, they are authorizing an outside existence to control them. True power, though, is always held within us. Behind the power of individual human beings, the energy of the Universe is actively working. Through our own will, we give instructions to that power, and it works according to the instructions received.

❧ *Insubstantial Power*

It makes no sense at all to just look at the power of this tangible, 'third-dimensional world'[5] and call it real power. What we have been describing as 'power' and exercising in 'power relationships' is far removed from the real thing. It is a distortion of real power.

This distortion occurred in people's hearts when they began seeing themselves as material existences and nothing more. This distorted 'power' must not be confused with true power. It is a dreamlike, phantom thing without real substance. Yet human beings have been focusing their attention on this insubstantial power and letting it yank them about in low-level power relationships.

Since it is unreal, why has this insubstantial kind of power not faded away and disappeared? It is because human beings keep adding more of their own power to it.

The only one who gives your power away is you yourself. You believe in external power and enslave yourself to it. Then you moan and grieve that you are unfree, that your hands are tied. Why do you give power to people, objects, or conditions in the outside world that originally had no power of their own to control you? You do it out of silliness. You do it because you have not grasped the truth. You do it because you believe that the power of other people or other things is stronger than yours or better than yours. You blindly believe that your power is no match for the power outside you.

Why do you think that your own power is inferior, or that you are powerless in comparison with others? It is because you have lost touch with your divine Self. You formed the idea that your own power is inferior because you have not yet encountered the truth of your existence.

People who have not wakened to truth think of power as being third-dimensional power, the power of the material world. Third-dimensional power, or material power, is nothing like real power. Yet in order to obtain this totally unreal kind of power, most people struggle and agonize through an entire lifetime.

Even if people obtain this unreal power for a while, what does it amount to? Does it mean that they will never experience illness or death? Does it guarantee that they will live their lives abundantly and peacefully? If this were the case, it would be all right for everyone to pursue that kind of power enthusiastically. But there is no such guarantee. Even so, mankind is fighting day and night over this empty kind of 'power'.

How much charm does this unreal power hold for people, that they will lie to themselves and betray others to obtain it? Does that power guide them to happiness? Does it uplift them? Does it bring harmony and prosperity to their lives?

The answer to all these questions is *no*. That type of 'power' brings a minus to human beings. People who obtain that sort of 'power' are exposed to uncertainty and fear, and become entangled in struggle and killing. Not only they, but also the people around them have to make forced sacrifices and tumble into misery.

The Force of Negative Thought-Waves

Why does this 'powerless power' bring misery? It is because it is made up of negative thought-waves, nothing more. It is composed of the mental energy of mankind's materially-oriented attachments, desires and struggles. It is energy that has been poured into something with no original substance. In firmly believing in that inharmonious 'power', mankind has caused all that negative energy to gather densely together and assume an identity of its own.

The thoughts of even one person have the potential to wound others or entrap them in misery. When you multiply this by the volume of thought-waves emitted by the several billion people presently living in this world, and then add the accumulation of thoughts emitted since the beginning of human history, what is the result? What was originally an empty, unreal power has been fuelled by the concentrated energy of mankind's thinking, and has billowed into an energy source of colossal proportions. This kind of 'power' is leading mankind to misery, and is pushing it to the brink of destruction.

People who obtain this kind of 'power' come into sudden wealth, become influential, or live an ostentatious life of luxury. To the eyes of others, it looks as if they are living exactly as they wish to live. Few people recognize how precarious their situations actually are. In the short run, those people might indeed be enjoying an exalted position or living a life that is the envy of others, but as the power they hold continues to work for other people's downfall, sooner or later their own position or their own lifestyle is sure to crumble.

⤳ Changing Your Concept of Power

If all your attitudes are based on a belief in the various levels of power associated with present-day material society, true happiness will not come your way until you change your point of view. If you have firmly believed that strong power was held by things outside yourself, it is time to revitalize your thinking.

Look more closely within yourself. Have you even once noticed that a wondrous, brilliant power exists within you? Have you overlooked your inner power, being continually preoccupied with other people and other things? The more you focused on the outside, the more you were beaten down, and the more evidence you saw of your own helplessness.

You may not have been aware that the power within you has been constantly flowing into your body from the infiniteness of the Universe. Without freely utilizing this power, you may have let it sleep fruitlessly, envying others and comparing yourself with them. As a result, you felt inferior to others. Then, in order to hide your inability, and fearful of knowing the truth, you gave your power away to external things and

assigned yourself the miserable role of submitting to that
outside power.

Living this way makes people downright illogical. While
living in subordination to the authority that they turn over to
other people or other things, they experience the very same
anguish and sadness that they anticipate. They express their
feelings outwardly, describing themselves as being sad and
unfortunate. In effect, they are acting out a situation that they
have wished upon themselves. But they do not notice this.

∽ Do Not Wrestle With Yourself

If you are unaware of the power within you, the power relationships between you and others, put in concrete terms, go like
this: *I am no match for you. There is no choice for me but to submit
to your power. You outshine me. It can't be helped. Since I am powerless, it is out of the question for me to control my own behaviour. I
couldn't be expected to do that. So all I can do now is obey you, however much I dislike it.*

Though they may not be expressed in words or actions, if
thoughts like these have been released, the other party
will receive them. Then, through the energy of the thoughts
you have been emitting, the other party will unknowingly
behave so as to place you under their control, even if they did
not originally intend to dominate you or to vie with you for
superiority. You yourself have caused them to behave that way.

You might say, *No, I don't remember thinking anything like that.*
But you have had many thoughts that you do not remember.
Many of these thoughts were released from a past conscious-
ness, before you were born in this world.

When the other person actually looks down on you or
ignores you, you feel upset, angry and frustrated. You plummet
into misery, and though the situation originated in your own
thinking, you criticize the other person, saying they are at fault.
This is how you justify and console yourself.

You have been wrestling against yourself, that is all. It is quite a senseless story, but people are doing this unconsciously. Since mankind has not opened its eyes to reality, we are stuck with this state of affairs.

The power that we have been conscious of is scientific power, political power, medical power or the power of talent. We also recognize the power of wealth, knowledge, experience, physical beauty or physical strength. Or, we might perceive power in someone's family, birth, upbringing or background. People have been living with the conviction that these fragile kinds of power, belonging to an utterly low dimension, are a reality. From pursuing these kinds of power, human struggles have spread insatiably. In some way, everyone has experienced this and suffered from it. In extreme cases, people become self-destructive, cursing and tormenting themselves and denying even their own existence.

ꙮ *Take Pride in Your Divinity*

If things keep going this way, they will end in disaster. Human beings must wake up and see that each person has a magnificent, true Self that cannot be dominated by any outside power whatsoever. You need to be thoroughly aware that your value as a human being is not determined by the volume of your knowledge or experience; nor is it determined by your birth, riches or property.

You yourself are the reality. It is a mistake to assess yourself in terms of the knowledge or experience accumulated by your small self – your ego. You must never assess yourself in those terms. Your merits cannot be evaluated that way. A human being always exists within God Itself, not within knowledge or experience. Neither does a human being exist within the context of social custom, or the knowledge and experience connected with it. A human being is always a resplendent light, emanating from God and formed in God's image, holding limitless abilities. Whatever experiences mankind may have had so far, or whatever it might go through in the future, each person should steadily take pride in knowing that he or she is born from God, and should continue to live with dignity.

Each of us is directly connected with the Great Life of the Universe. Its infinite energy and power are always raining down on us from higher worlds. When seen in the light of this marvellous power, the prevalent 'power' relationships in this third-dimensional, material world become quite meaningless.

The unlimited power that is raining down on us is the power of divinity itself, urging mankind toward its awakening. Since it holds infinite energy, this power actively works in all areas and all fields of endeavour. It turns into all kinds of constructive, or 'plus' energy. It spreads out, becoming the power to lead mankind to peace, the power to lead mankind to happiness, the power to bring mankind into complete harmony. People who awaken to this unlimited power are the ones who will find true health, happiness and success.

⌒ Open Your Eyes

If you are now suffering, if you have come up against a thick wall, if you have been hit hard by illness, if you have been beaten down by heavy setbacks or are living without hope, open your eyes and look carefully. The different kinds of power that have come up against you are all phantom existences, nothing more. The strong power that presses down on you, the unseen power that binds you, the unexplained power that tries to crush you – none of those powers is real. They are powers that you constructed by believing in their existence.

How senseless it is to be led around and manoeuvered by that kind of power. On top of that, how preposterous it is to sink your life-energy into it, eroding your life away bit by bit, giving your own power to an illusionary 'power' then bending to the power that you gave away and gasping for breath as a result.

Right now, you have to see that there is no such power.

How silly it is to heartily believe in that 'power', heartily fear it and flee from it. Silly is not even the word for it.

You are a divine life, divided out from and directly connected with the Great, All-inclusive Life. Don't you realize that spiritual and divine power are overflowing from the Great Life Source and streaming into your body?

The 'power' that is afflicting you now is not rooted in reality. By stubbornly believing in it, you are giving strength to its existence. By continuing to think about it and pour all your might into it you are whittling away your own life-energy.

In the original, divine world, evil, illness, poverty, lack and loss simply do not exist. Such things are produced through illusions in the human mind, nothing more. As the whole of mankind throws its energy into those illusions, it makes them into something stronger. The more mankind thinks of poverty, illness and struggle, calling them to mind and fixing its attention on them, the power of those conditions only swells and solidifies all the more.

Conditions materialize according to human beings' thinking, and fear generates fear. This is the law of thought – the law of this third-dimensional world.

⌖ *The Power of Harmony*

For those who are turning toward truth, there should be nothing to fear. Everything that has happened so far is in the past. Those things were not done by the 'you' who has wakened to truth.

From now on it will be different. You shall not acknowledge power that has no substance. You shall not enslave yourself to it or fight against it. You shall ignore it steadfastly. What is the point of fighting against something that is not there? Why associate with something that is not there? What possible motive could you have for competing over something that does not exist? Stop and think about it. Do you intend to keep on fighting over a phantom power for ever and ever? Isn't that a complete waste of time?

Isn't there something else that you should be doing at this moment? As soon as possible, uncover your whole and complete divine Self and let it shine through your existence. Polish your spirit brighter and brighter, closer and closer to its original image. Do not be misled by the world of material appearances, but turn your mind's eye toward the world of the spirit. Material appearances belong only to the third-dimensional, material world, but we are spirits who live forever. The time to focus only on the physical body is over. We must waken and freely live our unending life.

Like it or not, the time is upon us when spiritual principles of peace and harmony must spread across the earth. The Universe is counting on you. Draw forth your wondrous, inner power. Reach deep into your mind and pray. Pray with your whole being. Pray to your true Self, calling forth the light of harmony that radiates from the God of the Universe. This is the power of brilliant energy that bends to no power in this world.

May Peace Prevail on Earth.

TRUE PRAYER

All over the world people are praying. They are praying in the manner of their own country, their own ethnic group or their own religion. People who do not belong to a particular religion or organization are also praying, each in their own way. The majority of people in this world are praying. When you think about it, the number of people who do not pray is extremely small; and even those few people who consider themselves 'non-prayers' are, at subconscious levels, making an invocation that is somewhat similar to prayer.

Prayer is something that mankind cannot live without – a necessity for human life. In its original sense, prayer is the fundamental condition that first enables a human being to live. It is the essential energy that permeates each embodiment of human life.

When we feel happy or overjoyed, we spontaneously wish to express our joy directly and offer thanks to someone or something. An inner, driving force motivates us to do this. This is prayer. Or, when gasping from hardship or beaten down by affliction, we are unconsciously driven by the need to hold on to something – this, too, is prayer. Prayer is a vibration that calls forth and awakens the original life-energy within us. Prayer is what reverberates thankfulness toward the origin of our spirit for bringing us abundant joy, fulfilment, or a flourishing life. Prayer connects us with our source.

Or, when besieged by continuing disaster, misfortune or sorrow, when we feel that we have reached the limits of our physical strength and abilities, unconsciously sensing a crisis, we turn to the original substance of our spirit in search of stronger life-energy or the power to overcome any difficulty. This intense appeal is the vibration that awakens the original life-power. This is prayer.

Prayer is an Awakening Process

Prayer, then, is not as we have been thinking of it. It is not a particular request for the fulfilment of our desires, the attainment of our ambitions, or the avoidance of unwanted circumstances. True prayer is the process that awakens us to our human identity as children of God.

This awakening process functions as people call to the inner Self, God, with the unconscious, spontaneous outpouring of expressions of wonder, or moans and words of grief. This is, fundamentally, prayer itself. As long as there is life in your physical body and you continue to exist in this material world, your prayer is naturally ringing out. But you may not have noticed it.

Prayer is the energy of life itself. Because prayer is reverberating in you, life exists where you are. When your life leaves this world, your prayer leaves too, for life and prayer are inseparable. They are one and the same in your true, original Self, a shining light in God's world, reverberating throughout eternity.

With the genesis of human life, prayer simultaneously came into existence, and there was no distinction between them. Gradually, though, these identical things became separated in people's minds, and nowadays most people have drifted away from the essence of prayer. Yet in truth, human life and prayer can never be separated. Deep beneath the conscious level, each person is praying.

Connecting With Our Source

Each person is praying, but the way of praying is often mistaken. When anguish, misfortune or disasters are perpetuated, or when people find their illness and disharmony unendurable or they cannot achieve mental comfort and tranquility, somehow their prayer is missing the mark and failing to connect with their true, inner Self.

Prayer is the means of drawing out life itself. 'Life itself' means life-energy: the pure energy of our true Self. As much as possible, we have to draw out the life-energy that flows endlessly from our source, the centre of the Universe (God). When we are able to freely utilize this abundantly overflowing life-energy, any affliction, any anguish, any illness can quickly be relieved.

Many people, though, do not grasp the truth of this. However hard they pray, they are unable to connect with their true life-energy, and their efforts bring little effect.

True prayer connects us directly with our inner Self, urging its awakening. It allows us to actually experience the reality that our true Self is the same as God.

Each of us is born from the source of the Universe, and shares in the infinite wisdom and creativity of the Universe. Once we understand this truth, we can call forth and awaken the abundantly overflowing, unlimited qualities that exist within us. Unlimited health, unlimited happiness, unlimited flourishing, unlimited joy, unlimited success, unlimited wisdom: all these are contained in our infinite life-energy. Therefore, once we grasp the essence of prayer, any affliction, sorrow or disharmony will instantly vanish from our hearts.

Focusing on the Centre

It will not do for us to keep praying in a mistaken way. Since the time when human beings first began to fix on a mistaken concept of prayer, human anguish, sorrow, struggle and illness have been perpetuated instead of coming to an end.

People have disconnected themselves from true prayer. And yet, because they fervently desire to break loose from their suffering, heal their illness or resolve their disharmony, they continue to earnestly pray in a misdirected manner.

This is just as if you have lost something in your house, and go outside to look for it. An article that was misplaced in the house should still be in the house. If you make an exhaustive search for it in the house, you will surely find it. But if you forget that you lost it in the house, and look for it in the endless area outside the house, however hard you might look, you could hardly expect the item to turn up. As long as you keep looking in the wrong place, you will never find it.

Then, in a flash of intuition, it suddenly occurs to you that you might have lost the item in the house. So you decide to search the house. At the moment when you decide to do this, your success is assured. It is as if the article has already been found. In the same way, people have been vigorously praying, trying to find prayer outside the 'house' of prayer. Consequently they have not yet been able to discover true prayer.

There are people with a serious and honest disposition who make much more effort and have much more patience than others. They undergo extensive, rigorous discipline, and inflict pain on their physical body to the limit of their endurance. Yet despite all this, they still cannot reach true prayer. Why is this? The focus of their prayer is off-centre. And since their focus is off-centre, however hard they seek the central point, they do not find it.

Prayer that is emitted from the centre is sure to return to the centre. Prayer that is emitted from off-centre will not return to the centre. It will return to its starting point.

A large portion of humanity has been exerting itself to little effect. People have been praying, but praying in a misdirected way. No matter how much we pray a mistaken kind of prayer, it is still a mistaken kind of prayer. A prayer that is aimed away from the centre cannot make the connection with true awakening. Though there may be a momentary rescue and a temporary escape from suffering, these are not the same as awakening to an unchanging truth. However earnestly we may dedicate ourselves to prayer, a misdirected prayer will not make this connection.

Pray in Positive Terms

Today, most people's prayers go something like this:

> *May illness be cured as soon as possible.*
> *May poverty be eliminated.*
> *May family disharmony be alleviated.*
> *May we not get into accidents or meet with disasters.*
> *May our business not go bankrupt.*
> *May we not fail our exams.*
> *May we not drop out of school.*
> *May we not suffer from cancer, Aids, heart disease, or senility.*
> *May wars come to an end.*

There is no end to the list of examples. The content of each person's prayers would vary to some extent, but I have the feeling that the majority of people are praying in more or less the same way.

What is it about the words of their prayers that are mistaken? Though there are differences among countries and ethnic and religious groups as to the methods and formalities of praying, the content of mankind's prayers is similar. In short, people wish to be rescued from the suffering, sorrow, misfortune, war, illness, hunger and calamities borne by mankind.

Yet even though a large portion of mankind have continued to pray so earnestly, how many have really been rescued? Though people have continued to pray for such a long time, has mankind been delivered from disease? Has mankind been rescued from unhappiness? Have wars come to an end? Have natural disasters been held in check? The answer to all these questions is *no*. What is the reason for this?

True prayer is not a prayer for the curing of illness: it is a prayer for the manifestation of perfect health in the physical body. True prayer is not a prayer for an end to suffering and sorrow: it is a prayer for the arrival of happiness, joy and abundance. It will not do to pray for an escape from accidents or calamities: instead, we must pray for the advent of peace and harmony. It will not do to pray that we will not be left alone: instead, we must always pray that love and pure happiness will come to us. It will not do to pray for an end to hunger, war, and natural disaster: instead, we must pray for the true awakening of mankind and for true principles to spread throughout the earth.

⌇ *It is Time to Wake Up*

With these concrete examples, I think that you are already getting a sense of what aspect of our prayers has been mistaken. Yes, our prayers have been mistaken: the focus has been placed on what is deficient. Our prayers have been generated from a negative point of view. They have been passive rather than active.

Negative prayers attract what is negative. The more mankind prays negative prayers, the more emphasis is placed on negative factors. And so, instead of being alleviated or coming to an end, negative conditions take shape in front of us in magnified proportions.

Looking back on the lengthy history of mankind, why is it that mankind's prayers have not all been fully received and brought to reality on earth? I think you can understand the answer to this question. Too many prayers were generated from a negative standpoint. How many millions, billions, no, trillions of times have people prayed that way? Negative elements have been accentuated, puffed up and magnified by the huge volume of negative prayers that have been prayed until now.

If mankind continues to pray in negative terms, negative elements will continue to build up and expand with tremendous vigour. And in the end, through the functioning of those negative elements, mankind will proceed pell-mell along the path that leads to ruin. People must wake up and realize this.

May illness be cured. May poverty be ended. May unhappiness, suffering and sorrow be remedied. May wars and natural disasters not happen. By continuing to emphasize minus-oriented terms like these when we pray, the force of those words, along with the energy of our prayers, will end up adding strength to current conditions of unhappiness, illness, suffering and hunger. This follows the principle that when energy is added to something, it increases all the more.

You might think that it would be better to change the words *May the illness go away* to *May the illness be cured.* However, the word 'cure' itself suggests that there is something defective in the essence of a human being. Within the words 'be cured' or 'be remedied', whether it applies to unhappiness, illness, sorrow or failure, there is the connotation of correcting something that is inherently wrong. So I think you can see that the idea of remedy or correction is also implicitly negative.

✑ *A Prayer for Children of God*

Why is it inappropriate to pray for illness to be cured? The fundamental point is that human beings are children of God, and are therefore brightly shining spirits living on and on through eternity. Spirits who are formed in the image of God should not be expected to suffer from illness. All human beings are originally perfect and integral: rays of shining light. Since praying for an illness to go away gives credence to the illness, prayer words like these are not compatible with the true nature of man as an infinite, complete existence.

People who are now suffering from illness, gasping under misfortune or anguish, or hovering between life and death in the midst of war or famine, and who truly seek deliverance, need to pray in a way that calls to and awakens their original identity as children of God. Instead of focusing on their hard circumstances, they need to direct their attention toward their original nature, which they have lost sight of until now and which has not yet revealed itself on the surface. They need to call forth their original self, their complete self, their shining, healthy self.

May perfect health be manifest. May pure happiness come about. May everything flourish. Complete harmony. Peace, joy and abundance. Success. Use words like these when you pray. Words like these express the nature of God. Health, infinite flourishing, complete harmony and happiness do exist in God. Prayers for these qualities will not fail to reach their object. Your prayers will reach the centre, your true Self, emanating directly from the infinite source of the Universe (God). And from there these unlimited qualities will flow back to you without ceasing.

As you can see, how you pray is important. If you pray in a haphazard way, it turns out to be a hit-or-miss event, like propelling a lot of little balls into a game machine. It has little effect unless you pray with a clear, unerring attitude – the kind of prayer that reaches your true Self.

I think that there are people who have lost faith in the effectiveness of prayer because, instead of bringing the desired results, their continual and fervent prayers have led to increased misery, disaster and illness. This can result from continually praying in a mistaken way for many years. Prayer, in its original sense, must be positive. True prayer puts the focus on the infinite nature of God. True prayer awakens people to the truth. The truth is that human beings are children of God.

It will never do for mankind to repeat the mistaken approach to prayer that they have taken until now. When we pray to God, we need to use good, positive words. Also, we need to seek only conditions that are whole and complete. From moment to moment it is important to focus our mind on qualities that are perfect and without limit, such as abundant health or infinite calmness.

⟜ *Prayer for World Peace*

May Peace Prevail on Earth. This prayer, emanating from the infiniteness of God, is a prayer of infinite life. It includes all our desires for the true happiness, peace and harmony of each member of humanity. It contains the essence of the true teachings and true prayers given to us by the great saints and teachers of the past.

May Peace Prevail on Earth. This is the epitome of a positive prayer. It encompasses each and every one of the people who now exist in this world, as well as those who have already passed away. It also embraces everything in existence: animals, plant life, minerals and all forms of life that have a God-given mission to fulfil. It is filled with thankfulness to everything – the sun, the air, water, the earth and all nature's gifts.

What is even more wonderful is that you yourself, as one life in humanity, are also included in this prayer. So when you pray *May Peace Prevail on Earth*, you are praying for the happiness, peace and the heavenly missions of yourself and everything in existence, all at one time.

It would not make sense to think that people who continually pray in this way would be strangers to happiness, would it? People who pray for peace to prevail on earth will definitely rise above their suffering. Each of them will waken to truth, without exception. The reason for this is that this way of praying attunes us to our divinity. When we intently pray for the happiness of mankind, absolute power and unlimited energy are brought out unceasingly from the source of our life.

Even if you use this prayer primarily for your own sake, it automatically connects with the happiness and peace of mankind. Because it is one with the harmonious vibration of the Universe, it allows all that is infinite to come coursing down on earth.

Until now, a great many prayers have been mistaken. The meaning of prayer has been largely misunderstood. In order to hasten the awakening of mankind, I am letting people know about the necessity of prayer for world peace on a wide scale. I am not doing it for my own sake; I am not doing it for yours. I am driven by necessity to spread true prayer for the sake of peace for mankind and peace on the planet earth.

We must not let people go on suffering more than they have suffered already. Mankind must not go on shouldering heavier and heavier burdens than it is carrying already. This earth must be swept clean of war, hunger and illness. In order for this to happen, each member of humankind has to awaken. In order for people to awaken, we must stretch out our hands in love. We must let people know about the importance of true prayer.

Many people are starting to recognize that things must not go on as they are. They are starting to see that a way of praying that is confined to a single religious or ethnic tradition will not rescue mankind as a whole.

⌇ *Time is Short*

This is what I always think: I have no right and no obligation at all to interfere with mankind, with any religious leaders, or with any prayer. Prayer is up to the individual and should be freely made by the individual. Whatever the prayer might be, when a person prays in real earnest, that prayer will definitely be heeded some day.

However, I would ask you to think about it this way. To invent the electric light bulb, Edison devoted a lifetime and exhausted all his efforts. From one invention to the next, from one discovery to the next, through repeated failures and after continuing days of anguish, he finally invented the light bulb.

It was a wonderful boon to mankind. But let me ask you this. Without being given that wonderful invention, if each person in the whole of mankind had tried, each in his own way, to invent the light bulb, wouldn't it have wasted an awful lot of time and effort?

It would be a mistake for each of us to spend all our lives trying to invent the light bulb. Even with a lifetime of effort, it is doubtful whether each of us would be able equal Edison's achievement.

However, those who simply accept and share in Edison's invention are able to enjoy the light it offers without putting forth the painstaking effort or the patience that it would take to invent it – to say nothing of using up an entire lifetime in the process. Thanks to their accepting attitude, they can spend their lives in a meaningful way. They can continue to live radiant lives holding wondrous possibilities. Why would it be necessary for each person to invent the light bulb in his own individual way?

It is just the same with prayer. If a wonderful, true prayer has been sent to this world, there are some who will accept and continually pray that wonderful prayer. There are others who will persist to the end in saying that they will discover their own prayer. Yet, being unable to discover a true prayer, they continue to pray in a mistaken way.

This is, of course, a matter for each person's free choice. But as present conditions continue, the peace of humankind is further and further delayed, and the number of awakened individuals remains small indeed. Meanwhile, the general membership of mankind remains unawakened and the energy of its negative thinking propels the world toward destruction.

∽ *May Peace Prevail on Earth.*

Because God is in a hurry for each member of humanity to truly waken, this true prayer has been given to the people of our time.[6] Whatever their faith, people all over the world can add these words to their own daily prayers. I feel quite sure that those who thankfully and seriously continue to pray for world peace are the awakened forerunners of humanity.

At this point in time, individual awakening alone is no longer enough. When we pray *May Peace Prevail on Earth* we are not praying for ourselves alone. We are not praying for our nation alone. We are praying for the complete harmony of everyone and everything. We are calling forth the infinite love, wisdom and power of the Universe and letting it spread out endlessly. This is true prayer.

May Peace Prevail on Earth.

Chapter 6

FROM MATERIAL TO SPIRITUAL CULTURE

D ay after day I can hear people's souls crying out for help: *It's no use!... How can I carry on?... Can't anyone help me?* These are the cries arising in human hearts today.

When we think about the progress made in scientific and technological fields, it would seem that life today should be easier than it was in olden times. We have been blessed with countless modern conveniences such as refrigerators, washing machines, vacuum cleaners, microwave ovens, and so on; thanks to cars, trains and aeroplanes, we are able to travel almost anywhere in a matter of hours.

With the technology of life-prolonging machinery or organ transplants, people can now live longer than they used to. Our life span has been extended, many epidemic diseases have been wiped out, and the infant mortality rate has declined. Since these circumstances are generally thought of as good for humanity, and nothing to be alarmed about, why must today's people experience such a suffocating feeling? In a world offering so many luxuries and conveniences, how can there be so many who cry out in distress?

➣ *The March of Material Civilization*

In my view, it is small wonder that people cannot breathe easily in today's society. This is because, by and large, the advances of modern civilization are limited to the material sphere. We live in a society where material goods themselves have become people's primary objective in life. Urged on by the insatiable desires of mankind, material development has been rushing ahead at breakneck speed. It has quite outdone itself.

Let us stop and ask ourselves whether our mental and spiritual progress has kept pace with the material. We could say that, along with the advancement of material culture, there has been some development in the human brain functions. But this development has been limited to the material functions. The development of our mental and spiritual functions has been left by the wayside. As a result, the job of developing our civilization has been carried on by the vigorous activity of our material functions alone.

The mental attitude that has guided the development of the earth's material culture has remained unchanged since olden times. If our spiritual development had kept pace with the material, we would not be hearing people's anguished cries today.

Nowadays there are people who live to be 90, 100, or more. Yet in our present-day material culture, we often find that the mind, which controls the body, shows little development after the age of 70 or so. In many cases, a person's conscious mental faculties seem to retrogress instead of moving forward. Sometimes their mental control keeps diminishing until it is almost entirely lost.

It must be painful to live in this world when our own will has slackened to such a degree that it is almost inactive. Yet in spite of this, medical science continues to devise ways of prolonging our physical life even further.

If our civilization is to evolve properly, it only stands to reason that our mental and spiritual development must keep one step ahead of the material. I say this because the material aspect is always directed and controlled by the mental, or spiritual, aspect. If the material aspect develops in advance of the spiritual, nature's balance is disrupted and the harmony between heaven and earth is thrown into extreme disorder.

This is why people today are crying out in distress. Material civilization has been rushing ahead so rapidly that people's minds are unprepared for it. As a result, they end up chasing round and round in pursuit of material goals such as wealth, authority, fame and material knowledge. Yet all the while, they know that they have neither the time, the know-how, nor the means to attain all those material goals.

The vast majority of the population cannot successfully compete for its material goals. While a tiny handful of people might succeed, the remaining masses are left merely desiring what they do not possess. As their material desires continue to mount, they become more and more anguished, more and more confused. They grow fearful and discontented, and in the end, wearied by their harsh ordeals, they lose hope and cast a dark shadow over their future. Meanwhile, heedless of those people's emotional anguish, material civilization continues to march forward, not knowing where to stop. Mankind's pleading voice is set aside for another day. Mankind's spirituality is left unattended to.

Society's relentless material advance has brought more and more disharmony, more and more illness, more and more struggle. This is precisely because it has not been accompanied by an evolution in mankind's spirituality.

∽ *Interaction Between the Ego and the Brain*

Because our development has been heavily biased toward material goals, we have diverted from our original purpose in life. We have been seeking unreal things, things without true and lasting substance. Having forgotten our intrinsic values, we are living in spiritual blindness.

As the ego continues to generate more and more material desires, the brain continues to upgrade its material functions so as to satisfy those desires. Mankind's material evolution has followed its present course precisely because of this interactive relationship between the brain and the ego. The brain and the ego have come to depend on one another. If the materially-oriented ego did not continue to produce a desire to do this or that, to attain this or that, to become this or that, human beings would not feel the need to cultivate the material functions of the brain. Material culture and civilization have developed, step by step, through society's all-out effort to satisfy the materially-oriented desires of its members.

To what point can we allow our material desires to continue escalating? If mankind itself does not curb its material desires, do you think they can be restrained by any outside force? Can the interaction between the brain and our material desires be halted in this way?

If mankind, in its misery, continues to escalate its material desires, there will always be those who will devise the means to satisfy those desires. The human brain will continually strive to cultivate its material functions, and as it does so, the ego will generate more and more desires. It is this repetitive interaction that has produced our present-day material culture.

The fruits of this process have been inscribed in our history, have they not? Yet has the mentality of struggle and conflict been resolved? Has illness been eradicated? Has peace come about? Do all hearts work together in harmony? The answer to all these questions is *no*.

⬧ Who Can Rescue Mankind?

Far from resolving these problems, we have to say that the development of material culture has brought with it more and more arrogance, more and more self-indulgence. We have witnessed such extreme brutality and coldheartedness that we would like to shield our eyes from it. Mankind is now enveloped in the raging waves of its own fierce desires and ambitions.

Even now, mankind remains unsatisfied. People today crave more and more; they aspire to more and more material advantages. How much more will they desire before their desires have abated? Are there any limits to their desires?

I would say no, not as long as human beings continue to live through the materially-oriented ego. The material ego itself knows no limits.

Will mankind continue in its present direction, letting its egocentric desires intensify to the point of its own destruction? Will human beings fail to waken to their spiritual identity? Will they continue to chase after material appearances and risk their lives for material attainments until they finally perish along with the things they have attained? If this is to be the destiny of humanity, does it not seem too miserable, too vain, too hopeless?

Who will put the brakes on the escalating desires of the material ego, that constantly act on the physical brain? This cannot be done by any outside power. It can and must be done by mankind itself. Not even God claims the right to curb or restrain the actions of mankind. Mankind is responsible for its own actions, even if they lead it to ruin. And since mankind's destiny is formed by each and every one of its members, each individual must shoulder his or her own responsibility.

As quickly as possible, all members of mankind must waken to their true identity. What is the point of remaining a prisoner to our egoistic desires? What is the point of being pulled to and fro like puppets, manipulated by the excesses of our egos? It is time to wake up to truth, now. At the earliest possible moment, we must waken to our true, spiritual identity. This is the way to halt the spread of mankind's insatiable desires. Mankind must waken to truth and put truth into practice.

For as long as mankind pays attention only to its material identity, its God-given freedom and creativity will be misused and misdirected. However, when mankind strives to call forth its inner, spiritual qualities, world conditions will change and the planet will advance toward harmony.

The General Public and the Experts

Here is the usual mechanism by which mankind attains its materially-oriented desires. Initially, individual members of mankind have no particular means of achieving their desires. They simply emit shouts, or appeals, expressing those desires. Next, their appeals are heard by scientists, physicians, physicists, mathematicians, and others who are leaders in their fields. The experts then strive to make the desired inventions and discoveries. Sooner or later, their efforts are successful. As a result, mankind's desires are met and satisfaction is achieved.

With this process, the members of mankind become linked together in strong profit-and-loss relationships between the general public and the experts. People look outside themselves for the fulfilment of their desires, seeking solutions from those whom they regard as superior to themselves and who, in most cases, pride themselves on the excellence of their achievements. Hence, the history of material culture has been the history of mankind's escalating material desires. However, if each member of mankind were to let go of his or her desires, there would be no further need for anyone to respond to those desires. In that event, the cycle would naturally cease.

The development of material culture and civilization has been a necessary stage in the earth's development. That stage has now come to an end. Yet through force of habit, people still attach themselves to their material identity and the profit-loss relationships that have been created between the general public and the experts. As a result, through industrious research, our material life span continues to be extended and mankind still remains unsatisfied. Its desire for physical longevity continues to escalate with no end in sight.

If we wish to live longer, why do we not seek the world within us so as to know the solemn truth of life? The truth is always one and the same, absolute and unchanging. The truth is always being conveyed to us via intuition, reverberating directly from our source.

Because we have let our lifestyle be dictated by the endless stream of materially-oriented desires associated with the external world, we have lost sight of our inner capabilities, the functions of the spirit. Instead, we have placed all our trust in materials. We have looked to materials for support and assigned power to them. Though the human spirit is far superior to any material, with a function unexcelled by any outside power, we have lost sight of it. In handing over all authority to material things, we, mankind, have allowed ourselves to be captivated, restricted and manipulated by materials. But mankind has not noticed this. Even now, it is earnestly pouring all its energy into further material development.

Mankind must not continue repeating the same mistakes again and again, stirring up the even deeper whirlpools of egocentric desire that churn in the recesses of its subconscious. We must not permit the further degradation of humanity. Rather, we must turn toward truth. By delving deeply within ourselves, instead of trusting in the outside world, we must become conscious of the limitless power within us.

✍ The Functions of the Spirit

Once you have rediscovered truth you shall never again be captivated by the enticements in the external world. In the world within you, there exist things far, far superior to any appearance of material development. When you become conscious of this, you will recognize the great wealth within you, finding things that are, as yet, uninvented and undiscovered in your material surroundings.

As you approach closer and closer to the source of your being, you will naturally become aware of the way to soothe or heal your illness. Your true, inner power will come alive. As feelings of joy and well-being spontaneously well out, you will be able to hear your inner voice of truth.

The only way to waken to truth is to seek it from within. If you seek it from the external world, it will only provoke an increase in your materially-oriented desires. If you know something from within you, it means you know something from within the Universe. It means that the principles of the Universe are becoming clear to you. This is because a human being is, in truth, the Universe itself.

We are enabled to live in this material world thanks to the outer garment, or covering, known as the physical body. Because of its material nature, this body is a finite existence. In spiritual terms, though, we freely live at all times through the limitless expanse of the Universe. Our true existence is great and mighty indeed.

Since the limitless wisdom and power of the Universe are within us, we can attain whatever we aspire to. Or, rather than saying 'attain', it might be more accurate to say that the things we seek are already present within us. If we tune in to our inner being, their shining existence will make itself known to us. Even if we cultivate the material functions of the brain, make all sorts of inventions and discoveries, and exert ourselves for the advancement of material culture, it cannot compare to the spiritual wisdom that abounds within us.

Humanity has hypnotized itself into believing that what we perceive on the material plane is reality. In truth, however, reality is found in the world of the spirit. Everything that manifests itself in the tangible world is the reflection of something from that unseen world. Everything that finds expression in the material world has been thought and created from the limitless capacity of the mind.

At the root of our existence, we know all that there is to know. When illness occurs, we know how to ease it. We know why it occurs. If we wish to live for a long time, we know how to do so. We also know that there is no need for us to keep our material body forever.

At the material level, mankind does not need to evolve further. In our inner world, a universe spans out endlessly, surpassing any level of material evolution. When we focus our mind's eye on what is needed, and centre our concentration on it, our mental energy works through the material plane and causes the needed objects or conditions to be realized.

⌒ *Olympic Athletes: Living Proof of Our Limitless Potential*

These days, when we see the feats performed in the various Olympic events, we can only gaze in wonder. Year by year, record times are getting shorter, and technical achievements are surpassing past boundaries. Whenever I watch the events in skiing, skating, gymnastics or the marathon, for example, I am deeply impressed to see the athletes striving to better their times or their skills.

Their moment of glory is, of course, truly spectacular, and when I reflect on the patient effort and stoic spirit that brought them to this point, I feel great respect for them. Many of these athletes are still in their teens. How many times, I wonder, did they feel like giving up their practise and enjoying themselves with others of their age? It takes a strong will and tremendous self-control to put forth so much effort day after day for the attainment of a goal.

The success of these athletes comes, I believe, from their efforts to draw from their limitless potential. This is not the kind of effort that relies solely on material aids. However helpful the various pieces of equipment and apparatus they utilize, they can do no more than offer support and assistance. In the end it is the athletes themselves who draw forth their limitless inner power.

Because they know that only they can tap their vast hidden resources, they train and control themselves far beyond the normal standard. Even if they have not glimpsed more than a tiny portion of their own capabilities, their efforts carry them beyond the current limits of human achievement.

These athletes are living proof of the infinite capacity of a human being. The more they focus on what is within them, the more they exceed our expectations. The more they strive to better their performance, the more they waken to their innate abilities. In this way, their mind unconsciously works to further and further develop their unlimited potential.

For the same reason I also enjoy ballet and the opera, and am continually amazed to witness the flowering of human talent. For example, when I see Odette in *Swan Lake*, I feel as if she were truly flying in mid-air above the stage. When the ballerina has awakened to her limitless capacity and is able to utilize it, she can poise motionless for a slightly longer time, and by doing this again and again she gradually creates the impression that she is not moving at all. Who knows how far this power of imagination may enhance our creativity in the future!

➣ Visualize Your True Self

In recent years, the practice of 'visualization' or 'creative imagery' has become widespread. A ballerina, for example, might visualize herself as a swan, and as she dances, deeply absorbed in becoming a bird gliding freely through the sky, she commands a power far greater than we would have thought possible.

What happens is that when we focus intently on an image, our repeated effort and training cause our latent abilities to surge forth and come alive. As we unconsciously attune ourselves to our capabilities, our power is increasingly drawn out. In many fields, this inner power is being exhibited more and more. Since this is one stage in the mental evolution of mankind, it brings me great happiness to see it.

The effects of creative imagery are far greater than we realize. When we concentrate fully, it brings us psychological relaxation, and from that state of relaxation new power comes coursing through. When we gather together all the diffused energy that we have been being scattering in various directions, and focus it on one point, its strength is intensified and it grows in volume. As a result, we can naturally manifest much more power than we otherwise would have.

Even if they do not know that the unlimited wisdom and capability of the Universe are inherent in each human being, artists and athletes call forth tremendous power and creativity. Just think, then, of the enormous effect to be achieved when we practise creative imagery based on a knowledge of our divinity!

How marvellous it is to visualize your true Self, holding all the infinite qualities of the Universe. Since your true Self has no material ego, it is none other than infinite love, infinite wisdom, and infinite life itself. It continues to emit love and life to your family, the people around you, to humanity and everything in nature, now and forever.

✏ *Manifest Your Divinity*

We each create an image of ourselves, an image that falls short of our divinity. It is extremely important for us to upgrade our own self-image until it coincides with the reality: that human beings are essentially one and the same as God.

Just by thinking about and visualizing our divinity, we can experience remarkable changes in our lives. If we have harboured a loathing of our spouses, we will find that our loathing has lessened. If we have been infuriated with our children, we will find that our emotions have quietened. If we have been tormented over problems in our jobs, we will find that those problems have evaporated. We will find ourselves able to forgive everything with a feeling of love and appreciation.

If you find it difficult to grasp the truth of your divinity, I would like to suggest that you start by visualizing yourself as one who is formed in the image of God. First of all, just hypothesize what it would be like to be one with God. You might think, for example, 'If I were God, I would not do things that way. If I were God, I would purify all negative thoughts, one after another. I would never blame myself for anything. I would radiate joy all of the time. My heart would be filled with abundant love, enthusiasm and vitality.'

As you practise envisioning what your true Self would do, it will turn into a habit. Such thoughts will purify your subconscious, and gradually, your mind will be transformed. As your consciousness fills with light, you will reach the point where you can recognize your true identity – your oneness with God.

After that, you can advance to the next step. You can let your divinity show through in your daily thoughts, words and actions. In other words, you will think, speak and act as God does.

To assist this process, continually remind yourself that you are as God is. Try repeating the following words to yourself time and time again:

I am as God is.

The words I speak are the words of God; the thoughts I emit are the thoughts of God; the actions I take are the actions of God. The words, thoughts and actions of God are abundantly overflowing with infinite love, infinite wisdom, infinite joy, infinite happiness, infinite gratitude, infinite life, infinite health, infinite light, infinite energy, infinite power, infinite success and infinite provision. They are nothing more, nothing else.

Since I am as God is, I speak God, think God, and put God into action.

I brighten and heighten myself, revealing only God, such that when others see me they are only able to feel that they have seen God.

Those who have seen me have seen God. I emanate light and continue to radiate the supreme, infinite love of God to mankind.

⤳ *From Material to Spiritual Culture*

In the very near future, mankind will waken to its divinity. We can do this, because there are no limits to what we can do. If there seem to be limitations, those limitations are an illusion. Since our lives radiate from the divine source of the Universe, the time will definitely come for us to freely demonstrate its unlimited power.

Material culture has come to its final days. From now on, we will be stepping into a period of mental and spiritual development. We are rapidly moving into an age when, without this awakening, humanity will not be able to survive.

If mankind's anguished cries for help are to be quietened, we must do our utmost to urge its awakening. Otherwise there will be no alternative but for mankind to be dragged down into the endless whirlpool of its materially-oriented desires.

As we near the end of material civilization, will mankind also come to an end? Or will we advance to the next stage? The answer depends on each one of us.

May Peace Prevail on Earth.

LISTEN TO YOUR HEALTHY HEART

Truly healthy people do not think about illness. Because they are healthy, they feel no anxiety over illness at all. They do their utmost throughout the day, and enthusiastically look forward to the work they will accomplish the next day. Without even thinking about it, they have confidence in their health.

If someone close to them becomes ill, they feel deep compassion for the person and try to help in any way they can. Yet they are able to think of that illness as being entirely unrelated to themselves. The thought that they themselves might become ill never crosses their mind. Even if they come in contact with people in the final stages of disease, their minds are never swayed by anxiety or fear. It is as if there is an invisible wall standing between them and illness.

Though illness is coursing through this world, if you are truly healthy you will never be influenced by those unhealthy vibrations. You will always see illness as something on the other side of the wall, unrelated to yourself.

Why do so many people take a strong interest in illness? It is because they have lost confidence in their own perfect health. Once you allow anxiety over illness to penetrate your heart, attaching yourself to the thought of illness, it means that you are losing faith in your health. People who think of themselves as healthy never fear illness – this is precisely why they stay in good health.

The moment you begin to worry about illness, your health begins to deteriorate. The fact that you are absorbed in building defences against illness proves that uneasiness and fear have crept into your mind. Truly healthy people have no fear of illness at all. Though today's society is flooded with information about illness, it never distracts them or captures their interest. They simply continue to go their own natural way.

Turning Healthy People into Sick Ones

Why have so many people lost faith in the natural health of their inner being? With the advance of material culture and civilization, human beings lost track of their whole and complete spiritual selves. As more and more people came to doubt their own perfect health, more and more doctors were needed, more and more medical facilities sprang up everywhere, and more and more medicines and pharmaceutical products were called for.

Who is responsible for this? Those responsible are the ones who have lost confidence in their health.

If this cycle continues, we can expect more and more new types of medical treatment to be devised in the future. And as more and more doctors and more and more medicines are produced, they will turn more and more healthy people into sick ones.

When presented with a continuing deluge of information on illness, even a robust person can begin to feel insecure. New information on illness is continually being provided to perfectly healthy people; and since those people look upon new information as the highest form of wisdom, their hearts are open territory for anxiety.

Fuelled by people's belief in them, illness and products

aimed at treating illness have taken on an authority of their own. They now march boldly through the world of healthy people. Illness, once confined to the other side of 'the wall', now has crashed through that wall. Its influence has spread to people who used to have confidence in their health. The wall has crumbled, and healthy people find themselves entangled in illness. While living in this present-day world of material culture, virtually everyone experiences some degree of apprehension over illness, whether great or small.

At the root of their existence, all human beings naturally live in perfect health. But today's people have lost all memory of this.

✎ How Does a Healthy Person Think?

People today have forgotten how a healthy person thinks. A truly healthy person naturally thinks bright thoughts all of the time. A truly healthy person speaks only words that emit waves of bright light. Since their minds emanate perfect health, such people never accept negative words, nor do they need to use them. Even though, on the other side of the wall, there are unhealthy people, or people with negative thoughts and actions, those living on this side of the wall remain totally unaffected. They ceaselessly create healthy thoughts and actions with perfect freedom.

When your heart is healthy, everything about you is fair and upright, loving, cheerful and harmonious. Bright light fills your mind and floods out from you. Without making any particular effort, you naturally emanate thankfulness toward everything that sustains your life and helps you to grow.

People with healthy hearts never feel hatred or jealousy of others. They never curse, harm or ridicule others. They cannot. They cannot even imagine doing such things, for such words and actions are possible only for people with ailing hearts. Once you find yourself taking pleasure in another's failure, wishing for another's misfortune or envying another's success, it is a sign that your heart is no longer in perfect health. Unhealthy vibrations have begun to creep in.

When your heart is in perfect health, you naturally say and do things that reflect your luminous, wholesome thoughts. You accomplish your work with zest and enjoyment, with new ideas pouring out one after another. You spontaneously feel that you are working not only for yourself, but for others as well. Since you strive for the benefit of mankind, the fruits of your efforts continue to multiply.

People with healthy hearts live spontaneously, without pretension. On the other hand, many people who have immersed themselves in material society have ailing hearts. They struggle and fight against others, curse, hate and kill others. They, too, once had perfectly healthy hearts. Their bodies used to be healthy too. But as their hearts gradually drifted away from good health, they consciously began to take an interest in physical illness at the same time.

When your heart is healthy, you wish to be in touch with nature. You long to be one with nature. Your thoughts are always airy and clear. You cannot help loving others, and are not content unless you can be thoughtful and helpful toward others. You live a positive lifestyle, your thoughts overflowing with bright hopes. You shun disharmony and strife, and love peace. You can intuitively sense the divine. Since you are aware of your divinity, you emanate thankfulness for all that enables you to live.

✍ *Your Healthy Heart is Your True Self*

No doubt you have heard the phrase *Human beings are sons and daughters of God.* This is just like saying that human beings were originally formed with healthy hearts. Essentially, human beings are not vastly different from God, as most people mistakenly think.

If you maintain a healthy heart, there is nothing to stop you from grasping the truth of your existence. Your healthy heart is your true Self, a current of life flowing from the source of the Universe. Your true Self naturally gives expression to all the unlimited qualities of the Universe: unlimited wisdom, unlimited energy and unlimited appreciation. You express them in thought, word and action without the least strain or difficulty.

Saints and sages are not the only ones who give expression to the divine. If you have a healthy heart, all your thought vibrations are composed of light and light alone. You understand who you really are, and your life resonates in tune with the harmonious laws of the Universe.

Our present world situation paints a picture of war, struggle, famine, epidemics and natural disasters occurring everywhere. We see no end of fear, distress, cruelty and cold-heartedness. All these conditions were caused when mankind lost its healthy heart.

Mankind is sick at heart, but when all people regain their original health, this world will naturally be filled with peace and harmony. A society and a nation made up of people with ailing hearts can only be unhappy, inharmonious and destructive, but a society created by people with healthy hearts is sure to reflect peace, happiness and prosperity.

The same is true for an individual. A way of life created by a person with a sick and injured heart is dark and miserable, but people with healthy hearts build flourishing lifestyles, overflowing with peace and happiness.

From the beginning, each member of humanity had a healthy heart. There is no one whose heart is originally unhealthy.

Fearing nothing, your healthy heart is conscious only of the light. You see the luminous qualities in others, in nature and in everything. Darkness is powerless when faced with light – it simply disappears. That is why your healthy heart can hold nothing that is dark and shadowy. All your thoughts and actions radiate exuberance and gratitude. You feel the joy, success and contentment of others just as you feel your own, for you see no distinction between them and you. This is because, when you are truly healthy, you naturally feel a sense of oneness with the Universe.

This is the natural state of each human being. Yet when your heart is ailing, what is natural is no longer felt to be natural. Everything becomes warped and twisted. The way you see and feel things and the way you communicate with nature is distorted.

The Truth is Reverberating Within Us

How can we keep our hearts healthy? Once our hearts are afflicted, how can we restore their health? Each of us must intently listen to the truth that reverberates within us.

Our inner Self is constantly supplying us with the exact information we need: the truth emanating straight from the heart of the Universe. Just as migratory birds flying in the great sky can aim precisely at their destinations, and just as young salmon that were spawned in a river swim to the sea and finally return unerringly to the same river, all lives are guided by the Universal Law. While living together in harmony, everything in Great Nature gives full expression to its God-given wisdom in tune with the universal design.

Human beings, though capable of discerning all there is to life and death, are oblivious to their limitless, divine wisdom. They ignore the directives of their inner selves and lead aimless, desperate existences, not grasping even the first thing about life and death.

Though many people are living their lives in all seriousness, they really understand next to nothing about themselves. Despite their earnest wish to live in love, happiness and peace, they deeply hurt themselves and others. They tell themselves that they do not wish to curse, injure, fight against or kill others, yet they are doing those very things in spite of themselves.

Why does this happen? Is it because the world itself is ailing? Or is it because each human heart is afflicted?

An unhealthy heart can only produce unhealthy words and actions. However you might try, however you might endure, an unhealthy heart can never bear healthy fruit. Your efforts can never get off the ground.

The first thing each of us must do is to rediscover our own healthy heart. We must recall what we once lost sight of – what still exists deep within us.

↷ Listen Only to Your Healthy Heart

Observe yourself closely. Remember a time when you breathed with flawless health. Focus on your true Self. Hear its voice. Do not ignore the divine voice that reverberates within. Tune in to it. Believe in yourself. Listen to the cry that is echoing from the depths within the depths of your soul. That voice of truth is the reverberation of your healthy heart. Joined with the source of the Universe, it is emitting the vibrations of truth to you.

Do not be misled by the cries of the egocentric thoughts that assail you. I can hear those desperate voices crying out for happiness, wanting to escape from suffering. I can hear the voices that shout: *I hate him! . . . He is torturing me! . . . I wish him bad luck! . . . How I adore my child! . . . I can't bear to see him like this! . . . My heart aches so, what can I do? . . . I can hardly breathe! . . . Take away my agony! . . . Take away my illness! . . . I wish I were in his shoes! . . . I want a house! . . . I want money! . . . I want to be president! . . . I want to be on the Board of Directors! . . . I want to be famous! . . . I want to be respected! . . . I want to be rescued from the suffering and the terror of illness!*

These are the cries and pleas that you keep emitting in your heart. Yet none of them comes from your true Self – do not fool yourself into thinking that they do. They are the voices of your illusory thought-waves, returning to you now from past worlds. They are returning to you from where they have been hiding – among the layers of thought vibrations piled up in your subconscious mind. They are emerging now, at the moment when they are meant to fade away and disappear.

Those discordant vibrations were produced by an ailing heart. Do not listen to them. They will only drag you down. Let them fade away, as they are meant to do.

Do you not notice another voice, resonating with clarity and freshness from the innermost depths of your being? Its vibrations are coursing toward you at all times, bearing the wisdom of your true Self. Each member of mankind, no matter who it is, has this inexhaustible wisdom flowing within, reverberating without inhibition.

If we consciously and calmly examine our hearts from a new perspective, we can awaken to that fine resonance, emanating from a place much further upstream than the voices of our desires. We can sense it cascading forth, vibrant with life-energy, abundant with all that is infinite.

⤳ *Your Healthy Self Can Come Alive*

When we listen to the voice of our healthy heart, we will be supplied with wisdom far surpassing the mountains of knowledge we have so painstakingly accumulated, even at the cost of our sleep. The absolute wisdom of our healthy heart holds information from every field imaginable: be it politics, religion, medicine, education, sports or whatever else, our true selves hold all the intelligence that human beings need. How sad it is that no one listens to this infinitely deep, inner wisdom! No one cares about it. There is not even one person who is truly conscious of the infinite, divine love shining within them. There is no one who has fully awakened to the brilliance of the absolute forgiveness radiating from their true Self. Yet even so, the bright vibrations of the true Self continue to surge forth, never pausing for an instant.

The voices of your surface mind and the voices of your

subconscious are the voices of desire. Never catch at them. Never think that they come from your true Self.

That was your mistake, wasn't it? You mistook the voice of greed for the voice of truth. Since then, there has been no end to your suffering, no easing of your sorrow, no cure for your malady. Will you go on this way forever, living like a puppet to your subconscious cravings – even while your healthy heart keeps calling to you and enfolding you with unlimited forgiveness?

Once you attune yourself to your healthy heart, you will notice things you have never noticed before. Problems that always overwhelmed you, however hard you wrestled with them, will suddenly be resolved by your healthy heart. The voice of your healthy heart brings you marvellous ideas that can be realized in an instant.

Since it resonates straight from the universal laws of harmony, your healthy heart can transform your present way of living. An ailing heart can only create an ailing lifestyle, but a healthy heart gives birth to a healthy life and a healthy world. A healthy life reflects the intention of the divine, just as it is. It brings our original, divine image, undistorted, into this earthly world.

Until now, you have been concerned only about what others could give you. This is only natural for an ailing heart. You have desired love, gratitude and forgiveness from your husband, your wife or your children. You have desired praise and respect from others. This is what the voice of your subconscious has been calling for. Those desires have manifested themselves in your words and your behaviour. From now on, though, you will sense a totally different resonance coming from your healthy heart.

You will feel like forgiving the person who seemed so hateful to you. The pleasure you took in other people's ill luck will fade and disappear. You will discover that you are turning into someone who can pray for other people's happiness with all your heart. Where you used only to seek love from others, you will now find a yearning to love others blossoming within you.

Until now, the negative side of you and others has always captured your attention. As this old habit disappears, you will find yourself noticing people's good side. Their luminous qualities will leap into view, and you will be able to discern perfection in them.

As you carefully listen to your healthy heart, your innately healthy self will come alive again. Even if illness should visit your body, you will naturally become aware of the way to heal it.

✎ Give Thanks to Your Body

Sit up straight, clear your mind, and pray for the happiness of mankind. Intently turn your thoughts toward the infinite: infinite love, infinite harmony, infinite potential and infinite life. Offer your appreciation to everything in nature that sustains your life: the sea, the earth, the mountains, food, water, plant life, animals, minerals, the air, the sun and all heavenly phenomena.[7] Deeply reflect on your inner truth – your divinity.

Finally, give thanks to each part of your physical body. Offer your heartfelt gratitude to your heart, your blood and all bodily functions. Give thanks to your internal and external organs, and to each cell of your body. Apply the palms of your hands to areas that are now sick, while sending them deep thankfulness.

As you do this, you may find that worry and fear keep pouring out of your heart. Even so, you should continue to praise and thank your body. You must closely question yourself to see which will be the winner: the voice of your subconscious or the voice of your healthy heart.

You must give the victory to your healthy heart. If you let yourself be defeated by the voice of your subconscious, you will never understand the meaning of your illness.

The contents of your subconscious are nothing more than

the lingering vibrations of your past thoughts and actions. Once a portion of it has come out and vanished, it will not return to you. As a result, things will surely improve. What you must do is to let those subconscious recordings disappear as quickly as possible. Never let your heart be shackled by the illness that is revealing itself now, at the moment of fading away. Do not attach yourself to it or fear it. Let go of it, naturally.

However relentless the pain, however severe the anguish, do not let it conquer your heart. Your pain and anguish, themselves, are evidence that your past errors are trying to erase themselves. If not through the pain, they would have no means of leaving you. Be grateful that they are clearing themselves out of your system. Be truly thankful for this opportunity to compensate for the debts you incurred in past worlds. Keep filling your thoughts with hope and gratitude to your body.

When you do this, it would be fine if you could scrupulously thank each organ and function one by one. At times, though, you might easily forget some of them. So as to have no cause for regret, you can simply think and pray: *Thank you, each cell that composes my physical body.*

This is similar to what we do when we think and pray: *May Peace Prevail on Earth.* This spirit of prayer encompasses not only you, but also your beloved family, friends, acquaintances, and the whole of mankind. In the same way, when you thank all your body cells at one time, you are thanking each and every one of your internal systems and all your physical structures – since all of them are made up of your body cells.

Believe in Your Healthy Heart

As you keep attuning yourself to your innately healthy heart, you will find many things becoming clear to you – things you had forgotten, things you did not notice or did not understand, or had left up to others. Gradually, you will come to comprehend them through your own power.

You will spontaneously know how you should respond to the situation where you have been placed, either through an inner hunch or through a flash of intuition coming from your healthy heart. You will know, on your own, whether you should recuperate in bed, or keep your body warm, drink something hot or cold, or let your problem clear itself with diarrhoea, and so on. No longer plagued with needless fear of illness, you will be able to cope with it calmly. (People generally fear vomiting, fever and diarrhoea, whereas in fact they are nature's way of removing poisonous elements that have accumulated in the body. These symptoms indicate that fatigue, contamination or excessive food and drink have been cleared away and the body perfectly cleansed.)

The best thing of all is being able to identify your illness through your own intuition, and knowing how to alleviate it on your own. You need not depend on doctors and medicines all the time. You can correct the illness that you created. In the end, no one else can do this for you. Your healthy heart can definitely find the way to heal it.

After scrutinizing your condition, if you feel that you need to consult a doctor for a diagnosis in order to fully manifest your self-healing power, you should not hesitate to do so. Medical facilities are also manifestations of divine love. Thus, with or without the help of doctors and medicines, you are ultimately meant to heal yourself with your own power.

It was you who attracted your illness, and you are also the one who will heal it. Though others can offer guidance and renewing love, no power outside yourself can heal it entirely. If you attain perfect calmness, you will recognize that you know your illness better than anyone else does. The 'doctor' who can best heal your illness is none other than yourself.

Since the general public is already sick at heart, they have not the slightest understanding of this truth. An ailing heart believes only in doctors. It has no means of knowing about universal principles. What an ailing heart believes in is a power outside itself. First and foremost, an ailing heart does not believe in itself. This is probably why your heart is afflicted in the first place.

Won't you try to believe in your own power, little by little? Please believe in the unlimited life-energy that flows within you all the time. Believe in your true Self.

Believe in your innately healthy heart. Restore it to its rightful place, as soon as possible. You can surely do it. Nothing is more wonderful than believing in yourself.

Everything that is in the Universe is in you. Only when you know this can you live your life with full confidence. This is the absolute truth: your inner being is one and the same as God.

When your awareness has reached this point, you will find that all disharmony has vanished from your heart. You will know that only divinity exists.

May Peace Prevail on Earth.

Chapter 8

DEVELOP YOUR POWER OF OBSERVATION

When you look at your family and the people around you, what do you see? Do you see them as radiant, wonderful people? Or do you see their faults and imperfections?

When we focus on people's shortcomings it puts us in an unpleasant mood. We find ourselves constantly getting irritated or upset. Sometimes we lose our temper completely. Why does this keep happening to us?

When we look at those who are close to us, and at other people too, we tend to see their imperfect side. And because we are in the habit of looking at their imperfections, their imperfections are the only things that come into view. This means that our power of observation is impaired – incomplete.

People who know about a human being's true identity constantly perceive the whole and complete person who lives within. They see everyone as a reflection of God – a child of God. Or, if they do not actually *see* that image of a person, they are *trying* to see it. They do this out of habit. They are always striving to see the inner, godlike nature of everyone. Their perceptive powers are geared toward what is perfect or complete.

Every human being is an extension of God, a vehicle of God. No matter how bad a person might seem on the surface, he or she is a vehicle of God. Every human being is naturally and continuously giving expression to God. This is what it means to live.

But at some point in time, we human beings stopped trying to see the true person, who gives expression to God. We became quite captivated by the part that had drifted away from God. Gradually, our attention shifted to that imperfect part, and we lost our original power of observation.

⤳ The Power to Distinguish Truth from Falsehood

As long as you lack the power to observe each person's true, divine nature that is constantly expressing itself from within, you will always be attuned to what is flawed or imperfect. As a result, flawed or imperfect images will keep appearing in front of you. When you perceive those imperfect images, you will feel displeased, hurt, or angered. But the disharmony that now exists in front of you is not within the object. It is within the subject: your own ego. The sole cause originates from your own loss of insight into the true substance of things.

This Universe, this planet earth and all living things are embodiments of God – expressions of God. Here, there and everywhere, God is breathing. God's wisdom dwells in everything. If you can sense this, it means that you are utilizing your true power of observation. You have the power to distinguish truth from falsehood.

Your power of observation is always being tested. At all times, through each and every image or occurrence that takes shape around you, it is being tested. When you are at home, or when you are walking along the street, all sorts of things are relentlessly leaping into view. At the instant when they come into view, you are distinguishing among them and making choices. What instantaneously selects some things and rejects others is your power of observation.

People who are equipped with their full power of observation discern only those manifestations that have true substance. They do not acknowledge things that are without true substance. They discard them immediately, without fixing their attention on them. And even if some of those things do come into view, they do not penetrate their mind. This process is naturally carried out from one instant to the next.

There are so many events and images occurring in front of us that if we let all of them invade our minds, we would be unable to get anything done. This is why we accept some and reject others. Usually, this process of accepting or rejecting takes place unconsciously. If we did it consciously, our nerves would be worn to a frazzle and we would be unable to do our work or live our lives. Our bodies would not hold up under the strain, not even for a day. And so, with our power of observation, we naturally and unconsciously carry on this selection process.

✐ Selecting Happiness or Unhappiness

Our power of observation is what gears our life toward happiness or unhappiness. Since they have lost their eye for discerning perfection, people with impaired powers of observation can see only flawed, fragmented images. And when we perceive imperfect images, conditions, attitudes or behaviour, we are not likely to feel well or happy.

Originally, though, a human being has total and complete powers of observation. Any human being can clearly distinguish what is perfect and harmonious from what is imperfect and inharmonious. We can all clearly and naturally judge whether our own thoughts, attitudes and actions are consistent with the unchanging laws of the Universe.

In its original state, a person's true mind is perfectly harmonized. If we come in contact with something inharmonious, we will have a feeling of revulsion. This is how human beings are made. We will spontaneously reject and turn away from what is inharmonious.

For our mind to be in disharmony means that we are not

following the laws of the Universe. This in itself is proof that we are out of harmony with Universal principles or the great, natural order.

A truly harmonious person is in tune with everything in the Universe and knows that we live because we are constantly receiving life from the Universe. This kind of person is aware of an unlimited, immeasurable quality that flows through everything and exists within everything.

From the beginning, it is a human being's inborn nature to be in tune with this infinite quality. This is because a human being is a child of God and has the nature of God. Every human being is continually reflecting God's image and giving expression to God.

This is why we must keep looking at the true, inner substance of other people, which is whole and complete and continually gives expression to God. We must never turn our eyes toward the side that shows imperfection. When we look only at people's true substance, our true powers of observation are being utilized. Even though the words and actions of our husbands, wives, children or the people around us may not be reflections of God, when we use our proper powers of observation, we can discern the divinity hidden beneath the surface.

At some point, though, we forgot our ability to see the whole and complete self within each person. Our hearts were overtaken by the faults, the ugliness, the deficiencies and the discord that emerged outwardly. We quite lost track of our power to see the shining figure that lives within.

On the surface of the sea, there appears a chunk of ice. Beneath it lies a gigantic iceberg, sparkling with mystery. But we believe only in the piece that appears on the surface, and cannot see the true, wondrous form that spans beneath it. We are mistakenly convinced that the small, surface portion is all there is.

When we look at a human being, we have to look at the whole existence, not only at what appears on the surface. We have to be mindful of the true existence that is hidden from view, and keep trying to see it. Every human being, without exception, is giving expression to God. To the extent that you are giving expression to God, you will definitely be able to discover God within other people.

med.

⌒ See Perfection in the Other Person

In order to discern God's image in others, we ourselves have to give expression to God. A human being is, originally, a medium for expressing God. When we are giving expression to God, we are reflecting our original, true image.

Though you and the other person are fellow human beings who continue to give expression to God, somewhere along the way you each lost your ability to perceive the images of divinity. This is why your suffering, your sadness and misfortune have not yet come to an end.

narr.

When you see your husband, your wife, your children or the people around you, why do you not try to discern the inner person, who is giving expression to God? Why do your eyes move only to the untrue part? If your present mental state is unbearably bitter and painful, what is the cause of it? Could it be that the other person is unable to give you the things that you yourself are seeking?

If so, why do you seek those things from another person? Is it not you who creates the things you wish for? However you might seek them from another person, they will not be attainable. They are not something to be asked for from another person, and they certainly cannot be attained by compelling another person to give them to you.

Have you been seeking love, joy, happiness, success, prosperity, health, talent and riches from another person? Have you been thinking that someone else will provide you with these things? When the other person has been unable to do so, have you felt angry and resentful? Have you felt like grumbling and complaining? Have you been critical of the person's character, personality and abilities? When your hopes, dreams and ideals have gone unfulfilled, have you said that it was someone else's fault? Have you pushed the responsibility away from yourself?

Do you say that your disappointment occurred because you married the wrong person, or because your children turned out unsatisfactorily, or because your boss showed poor judgment in people? In saying these things, do you vent your indignation by belittling those around you?

If you seek happiness through marriage, do not expect your happiness to be provided by your marriage partner. Your pain and your dissatisfaction will only increase in proportion to the degree of your expectations. Why is this so? It is because your partner has neither the duty nor the right to bring you happiness. Your partner has his or her own life to live. *Your* happiness will always be built through your own power. Neither your spouse nor your children have any obligation at all to satisfy your expectations or to fulfil your hopes and dreams.

Yet when their expectations are unfulfilled by others, people describe themselves as being sad and unfortunate. They say that their lives are dismal. But their unhappiness is not the fault of their spouses or the people around them – it is just that they presently lack the insight to discern the inner, godlike nature of those people.

When you see wholeness and perfection in the other person, when you sense that God is being reflected there, when you bless and praise them for this, the wonderful qualities of both parties will be brought to the surface. This, surely, is what makes a true marriage: to recognize the true, whole person who exists spiritually in your partner. It is to elevate one another and let each other's luminous qualities come shining through.

⤳ *Melt into the Divine Wavelength*

Think about a person whom you consider to be happy. It might seem as though their every wish is being granted by the people around them. Perhaps you believe that this is what makes them happy and contented. On the surface, it might look this way to everyone, but this is not the reality.

A truly happy person is not given happiness or success by someone else. A person who is living in peace and serenity is not simply benefiting from conditions that were arranged by others. A person who is surrounded by warmhearted people, and leads a bright and active life, is not in a situation that was offered to them from the outside. All those things were attained and created within their own heart. They won those things with their insight for discerning truth.

Truly happy people have been continuously manifesting their divinity in their daily lives. This puts them mentally in tune with others who have been living in the same way.

Truly happy people clearly understand that God is omniscient and omnipotent. They are also aware that they are the children of God. They believe that, since they are the children of God, they can manifest infinite divine wisdom and capabilities, just as God does.

When people come to understand the essence of this logic, their words and actions naturally melt into the wavelength of God. Because they are always mindful of God's infinite bliss, infinite flourishing and infinite success, they draw God's infinite energy and power toward themselves. They never expect to have their hopes and dreams fulfilled by someone else, or their happiness given to them from the outside. They just strive intently to bring out their own inner qualities.

We must each make the effort to express our own infinite qualities in our words and actions. Gradually, this will become a habit. Finally, we will become conscious of the perfect and complete being that is innate within us. By means of the wholeness and perfection that we are emitting, we will acquire the insight to perceive the whole and perfect images of our husbands, wives and children. When we reach this stage, all the images we attract will be whole and perfect. Happiness, success, health and ever-increasing abundance will be drawn toward us unceasingly.

Your Feelings Will Be Mirrored Back to You

As you continue to see only wholeness and perfection in others, you will come to treat them accordingly. For example, let us say that there is someone who tends to incur people's dislike. He gives them a disagreeable feeling, and causes them to feel irritated. He is spoiled and wilful, with an intense desire to express himself. Yet strangely enough, when he is with you he exhibits none of these traits. In your presence, he is filled with goodwill. Why is this? It is because you see him in an entirely different light from the way others see him. You see only his good side, and you treat him accordingly.

On the other hand, if you always get an unpleasant feeling from someone, or feel uneasy, insulted or wrongfully treated by them, you would do well to carefully examine your attitude toward the person. Somewhere, there has to be a mistake in your approach to them. In some way, you must be viewing them with hostility, fear, contempt or mistrust.

If you cannot conceal your uneasiness, irritation or mistrust of a person, your feeling will be transmitted to them. Always remember that what you see in the other party is a reflection of your own thoughts and feelings, whether past or present. Those thoughts and feelings will be mirrored back to you.

Imagine that you gave something away, free of charge. You did not expect anything in return. Yet though you did not wish to, you later had no choice but to receive something back.

If you give, you will receive: this is a natural law. The words and actions that you have released will find their way back to you, and the discordant or imperfect feelings that you have sent out will also be returned. The cycle is completed in this way, following the laws of nature.

Whatever kind of person he or she might be, the other party is in some way giving expression to God. Unknown to the world, they might be performing actions of charity and goodwill.

As long as we live in this physical, material world, it is extremely difficult for us to emit a bright light to others at all times. But the reverse is also true. However bad a person might seem to be, it is impossible for them to continually express evil, and nothing but evil, from their birth until the day they die. Even a villain protects and supports others, in a villain's own way.

Your attitude and the way you treat people can enable them to call forth their divinity and change their behaviour to any extent. When your treatment of others springs from the spirit of love, they will respond to the love you have shown them. Whoever they might be, they will surely respond to it.

When someone is nice to you, or thinks kindly of you, it means that you previously showed the same kind of attitude or feeling toward someone. If you show contempt to someone, if your attitude is overbearing, or if you make fun of them, sooner or later the exact same kind of attitude will surely be returned to you. Sometimes it will come from the same person, and there are also times when it will come from someone else.

Anyone and everyone, whoever it might be, is continually giving expression to God. *Life* itself is God. To *live* means for each individual to give expression to the *life (God)* that has been received.

You cannot live on another person's behalf and give expression to their *life (God)*. No one else can live on your behalf and give expression to your *life (God)*. No one can teach another how to give expression to their own *life*, nor can anyone be taught how to do this. Each of us has to pour all our energy into giving expression to our own *life (God)*. Having received our life from the one, absolute source, we each have the mission of letting its flame burn brightly in this world.

This is our one and only purpose in life. Day in and day out, we must pour all our energy into expressing divinity in word, thought and action. Only when we do this are we truly alive.

➥ *The Arrows That You Have Released Will Return to You*

How do you respond when your spouse, your children and all the people around you constantly confront you with their anger, discontent, fear, insults, antagonism and other disagreeable emotions? You must never blame them or be upset with them. The thing to do is to compose your thoughts and pray.

The other party's irritation and discontent originated from your side. If there had been no contact between you and the other party, the other party's anger and discontent could never have been generated. When you and the other party came into contact with one another, some sort of emotion surged forth in the other person. If, by some chance, the two of you had not met on that occasion, the other party would not have experienced those unpleasant emotions, and you would not have been obliged to receive them.

You yourself have always shot an arrow beforehand. The person struck by the arrow sends it back, carrying their own emotions with it. This is a law of the third-dimensional, material world. A poison-tipped arrow is reciprocated with a poison-tipped arrow, and an arrow of bright light brings back an arrow of bright light in return.

Therefore, you need not worry or blame yourself when you sense that others are treating you with hostility, resentment, or other negative emotions. The cause of these emotions may have originated long ago, in a past consciousness which you do not remember. They are emerging now so that their cause can dissipate and vanish.

Whatever unpleasant things might happen, just let them fade away and disappear on their own. At the same time, keep focusing on a concept of large-scale harmony, as in the words *May Peace Prevail on Earth*. Keep reminding yourself of the complete, renewing energy that flows without limit from the source of your being. This is how you train your mind to give expression to God.

As we keep living this way, always taking the viewpoint of large-scale harmony in our words and actions, we allow everything to be reconciled. We allow everything to come together in harmonious relationships. As we consciously try always to express harmony and wholeness in our words, attitudes and behaviour, incomplete and inharmonious things naturally fade from our surroundings.

As you continue to love others and feel appreciative of everything in God's creation, your own mind will be uplifted, becoming one with God. When you realize that you are one and the same as God, an indescribable feeling of happiness and calm will abound within you, and limitless joy and thankfulness will overflow from your heart.

If your own mind is always bright, continually emitting only love, you will not be harmed by anyone else's actions. No matter how fragmented and inharmonious, no matter how far removed from God those actions might be, you will experience no anxiety or fear, nor will you be placed in danger. This is because the other person lives in their own world, while you live in yours. Your worlds do not meet; your mental waves do not match. What influences the other person is their own thinking. Since it pertains only to that person's world, it will not affect you at all.

Polish Your Own Soul

If you are constantly being swayed by what other people think, say or do, if other people make you lose your composure and suffer dire agonies, it means that your surface mind (consciousness) is still in a fragmented condition. It is not yet functioning in its natural, healthy state. You are still looking to other people instead of looking within yourself. Your mind is still separated

from God. When you discover divinity in your own heart and give full expression to it, God's perfect, all-encompassing love will be yours. If agitation should filter in from the outside, it will be dispelled in an instant.

If, right now, you are in a sad and painful situation pertaining to your husband, if you are plagued by feelings of anger, resentment and discontent on account of your wife, if you are in the depths of despair, anxiety and fear over your children, you have to recognize that your husband, wife or children did not put you in that position.

If, at this point, you wake up and make a change in your words and actions, letting them continually reflect God, which is Good Itself and Love Itself, all the personalities that appear in front of you will be on a plane suitable to your own. Your formerly odious and unloving spouse will gradually change. As you change, the other party will change also. If you simply wait for them to change first, there is no reason to think that they ever will.

If neither of you changes, and the two of you go on loathing and quarrelling with one another, what will it leave you with? You will end your lives in the same ailing condition that you are in now. Wouldn't that be a futile way to live your life?

Others are others, and you are you. Just focus on uplifting your own soul, and yours alone. Polish your own character. Heighten your own spirit. Strive to waken to reality, as soon as possible.

Foster your true power of observation. Until now, you have been focusing your thoughts, energy and sensitivity on other people's unsatisfactory traits. Turn your thoughts around by 180 degrees. Expend your energy on bringing out your shining, healthy disposition and giving expression to it. This has nothing to do with other people. You need not meddle with other people. You must waken to your own truth, without a moment's delay.

If you do so as of this very moment, you will surely be free from all your suffering, all your pain. As you keep drawing out your own divine life, your marvellous qualities will develop and expand.

Until now, the majority of mankind have no doubt been thinking along these lines: *No one knows how much I have put up with until now. No one knows how much I have sacrificed. No one knows how I have exerted myself on behalf of my husband, my wife or my children.* Actually though, if they intently scrutinized their own thinking, it would become clear to them how much more they had been exerting themselves to satisfy the demands of their own ego.

Deep within us shines the image of God. Remember this, and you can develop your true power of observation.

May Peace Prevail on Earth.

Chapter 9

DOUBT

Doubt. Mistrust. Suspicion. At the moment when these thoughts cross your mind, your heart is rocked by violent emotion. Such is the fierce tenacity of doubt that it knows neither sanity nor reason.

Doubt attracts doubt. If you leave doubt to its own devices, it spreads out further and further, gathering impetus as it goes. When doubt takes shape in your mind, never be careless enough to let it run about unchecked. Once it has fuelled itself, it will rapidly expand its territory until it becomes too late to contain it. If it takes control of you, you are the one who will suffer.

You doubt God. You doubt others. You doubt yourself. And what profit does it bring you? None at all. It brings only despair and self-ruin. For doubt is negativity – a thought that is separate from God. Once you start feeding doubt, it will never stop growing. It will overrun your world.

Doubt is a disease, an activity that runs counter to truth. People doubt their husbands, wives and children. They doubt love, health and all the possibilities before them. They doubt themselves, their own hopes and their own abilities. They even doubt truth itself.

The people are mistrustful of politicians, and politicians are mistrustful of the people. Managers are suspicious of the workers, and the workers are suspicious of management. Doctors suspect illness, and patients are suspicious of their doctors. Everyone doubts someone or something. Until mankind rids itself of all doubt, it will go on suffering in mind and body. Doubt brings us no advantage at all. It only obscures the truth. It only destroys.

Doubt is the Source of Karmic Thinking

Do not waste your time on doubt or give your energy to it. Doubt is what took shape when we forgot how to believe in truth – stopped attuning ourselves to God. Doubt is the absence of purity, trust and truth. People who doubt have given up their freedom. Their doubtful thinking is what binds them.

Free yourself immediately from doubt. Do not relinquish your power to something that did not exist to begin with. People who doubt are sure to suffer. People who doubt cannot waken to truth, and are headed for misery.

This is because in the true world, God's world, there is no such thing as doubt. Doubt cannot exist in the midst of Great Harmony. Doubt cannot exist in the midst of wholeness. Doubt is what took shape when human beings wrongly identified themselves with darkness.

People doubt others and suspect them of thievery. They suspect themselves of being ill. They suspect that their work will end in failure. All doubts, whatever they may be, are the sources of karmic thinking, and they are the ultimate form of negativism.

The best thing a human being can do is to tune in to truth. We must each call forth our ability to recognize truth and trust in it.

No matter how things may seem on the surface, the fundamental truth remains unchanged: human beings originally come from God. We are originally whole and complete, and are always evolving through the laws of Great Harmony. We are always progressing toward oneness with our source. When we forgot this, we created the illusion called 'doubt'.

Once doubt has germinated, it can only grow. It grows as we concentrate our energy on it. The more we doubt, the stronger our doubt becomes. This is why we must uproot doubt in its early stages. After we plant the seeds of doubt, they will surely multiply.

If we let doubt grow in our hearts, it will crop up in the world around us, filling our days with pain and setting in motion a never-ending chain of troubles and complications.

⌁ To Doubt is to Reject Divinity

When the last traces of doubt have vanished from each human heart, how happy we will be! Mankind will know peace for the very first time. Soon, mankind must take an enormous evolutionary leap toward large-scale harmony and great development. To do that, we must recover our natural wisdom and innocence. Just like guileless children who wholeheartedly trust in the love of our parents, each of us must recover our belief in the innate goodness of all people. However bad a person may seem on the surface, we must not accept the badness as reality. We must believe only in the intrinsic divinity of one another. As we live toward this aim, true peace will settle into each person's heart.

In truth, human beings are one and the same as God. You are as God is. Others are as God is. Mankind is as God is. When all our thoughts flow in tune with this fundamental truth, not a single doubt can take shape in our mind. When all human beings discover divinity in one another – and also seek the truth of animals, plants and other forms of life – all living things will find perfect expression and live together in harmony. At that time, each of us will again be able to put our trust in humanity.

We must each do our utmost to banish all traces of doubt from this world. The first step is for us to stop doubting ourselves. If we doubt ourselves, our doubt will go on reinforcing itself until it turns into concrete reality.

Stop doubting your ability. Stop doubting your health, your character and your personality. Stop doubting your faith. Stop mulling over your doubts about every little thing that you have done in your life.

Your doubts may or may not be valid. After all, doubt is, by its very nature, nothing more than a hypothetical condition. Surely it is foolish to set in motion all manner of petty, negative thought-processes over something that has not even been proven true. What a waste of your precious time and energy! An enormous quantity of energy is condensed into the single activity known as doubt.

Doubt is profanity. To doubt is to reject God and to defy your own true Self. There are no limits to the destructive force of the negativism known as doubt.

What makes human beings so doubtful of everything? Doubt stems from a lack of self-confidence. There is not enough true human courage welling up in our hearts. Somehow, something is missing. When a person is fully confident, overflowing with healthful energy, untroubled by any thought of imperfection, there is no way for doubt to arise. Doubt raises its head when we are weakened, low on energy and prone to negative thinking. When our thoughts are fully facing the light, affirming our divinity, no doubt can penetrate our mind.

This is why I urge you to reject all dark and negative thoughts by swiftly exchanging them for waves of brilliant light. Banish all doubts by steadily sending out radiant thoughts. Keep thinking: *Infinite love – May Peace Prevail on Earth! Infinite harmony – May Peace Prevail on Earth! Infinite health! Infinite success! Infinite possibility!* Repeat these words strongly in your mind – or say them aloud when you have the

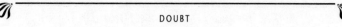

chance. Let their powerful energy strike out every trace of negativism. Begin as soon as you wake up in the morning and continue until you go to sleep at night.

If you continue in this way, striving to attune all your thoughts to your shining, inner Self and deeply appreciating the truth of your own divinity, there will be no dark space left where doubt can set in.

ᕃ *How Can You Cope With Doubt?*

What should you do if you suddenly discover that doubt has crept into your mind? Do not be alarmed, frustrated or down-hearted, but calmly and accurately assess your doubt for what it is. Do not make wilful, one-sided judgments about things that have not yet been verified. Do not sink into misery and despair, angering yourself and hating others on account of something that is still in the realm of conjecture.

The first thing to do is to determine whether your suspicion is borne out by fact. There is no point in dilly-dallying hour after hour and day after day. You would only be prolonging the matter out of weakness or lack of courage. You would simply be hiding from your fear that the facts might not match your expectations.

Doubt is an emotional thought that occurs when you are anticipating something bad. When you have a hopeful idea or feeling, you do not call it a 'doubt'. When you harbour fear and anxiety, thinking that your hopes will be disappointed, you cannot call up the courage to ascertain things on your own. It hurts your mind and body to spend your days in doubt, taking no steps to confirm the facts. Make up your mind to take action, in the way that is most suitable for you.

Keep it in mind that until you confirm the facts and clear up your suspicion, your doubt will never go away. Remember that if you go on spending dismal days shuddering with fear and anxiety, it will only magnify your suspicion, causing it to solidify all the more. It is no easy matter to lead a smooth and tranquil life while suspicion smoulders in your heart. You might think that since your suspicion concerns you alone, it will go unnoticed, but its influence cannot help spreading to your family and the people around you.

◌ *Compose Your Spirit*

Let us suppose that you are a wife who suspects her husband of being unfaithful. What are you to do? You might consider simply asking him about it. Instead of tossing the question back and forth, wondering if you should wait until you have got proof of it, wondering whether you are merely fighting with windmills, it might be better to put the question to him straightforwardly.

In some cases, the husband might answer untruthfully. If that happens, you can begin to think about your next course of action. Either way, your first step should be to resolve your suspicion quickly one way or another.

If you learn that your suspicion was groundless, you will realize just how much energy you have wasted. Once the burden of doubt has been lifted from your shoulders, how much lighter you will feel! The longer you leave your suspicion to fester, the deeper your wound will become. Even if what you suspect is proven accurate, your recovery will be quicker if the time spent doubting was short. Once the facts are known, if you have trouble deciding what to do next, you could then seek sound advice before reaching a decision.

The same holds true if you have doubts about your health. If you are feeling unwell, and think that you might have a particular disease, why not see a trusted physician and confirm it? Whatever the subject, the only way to resolve doubt is with an act of courage. If you have enough spare time for making excuses, you would do better to use your time learning the facts without delay.

If you visit your doctor and learn that your doubts were unfounded, you can thank heaven for it. Or, if your doubts are proven real, you can be grateful that you learned the facts in time. Either way, your doubts will be set to rest, and you can focus on composing your spirit.

If it turns out that you are diagnosed as having the disease that you dreaded, then consider your alternatives. Perhaps you will face new doubts: *Will I recover? Will I suffer a lot? Will it end in death? How much longer will I live?* and so on. If you feel this way, you must take courage and face your situation. Accept it for what it is. When you try to look away, when you try to run away, doubt turns to fear. Doubt must be dealt with on the spot. Though your problem may seem tremendous, fearful and very serious, if you delay facing it even for one day, you will suffer that much more.

You may confide your anguish to another, and receive words of compassion and advice. This may certainly console you for a while. Yet in the end it is you who must tackle your doubts. No one can do it for you. You must resolve them by your own power.

Do not say that you lack courage for you know that your doubt can be resolved by you alone. The longer you delay, the deeper your wound will be, and the greater your anguish.

⌒ *Do Not Make Your Doubts Come True*

Wouldn't it be wonderful if we could accept our circumstances without the slightest fear or doubt, never worrying *Oh, what will become of me now?* Ultimately, we can each live this way. We are meant to live this way.

Doubt itself is a concentrated mass of colossal energy, forceful enough to unhinge your life. Needless to say, you are better off without it. Yet if you are burdened with doubt, it is no easy matter to overcome it when you do not understand what it is or what steps are needed to dispel it.

As soon as doubt appears, do your best to clear it away. This is your first step. Once you have done this, you will naturally be able to guide yourself to the second and third steps through intuition and inner wisdom. Just as the earth evolves through the principles and laws of heaven, you will naturally be guided toward a solution. Quiet your thoughts and pray.

Since doubt does not exist in the world of your origin – the world of God – it can only have been created with your own thoughts. I ask you to plant this fact firmly in your consciousness. Doubt came into being the first time you reached a hasty conclusion about something. With neither proof nor verification, you made a snap judgment and doggedly believed in it. Over and over again, your blind belief gave rise to numerous struggles and complications, mushrooming out of control and putting you in difficult straits. It all started simply because you jumped to a premature conclusion.

Blind belief is dangerous beyond measure. Through the law of thought your blind belief gathers more and more energy, constantly reinforcing itself until, in the end, it grows into concrete reality and manifests itself in your world.

Why does doubt turn into concrete reality? It is because you put no effort into resolving it, and keep adding to it day by day. In heaping doubt upon doubt, you are tirelessly and relentlessly trying to make your doubts come true. Doubt turns to 'reality' because you continue to doubt day after day, again and again.

By constantly mulling over your doubts, you feed them all your energy. Even if there is clear evidence that your doubts are groundless, your concentrated mental energy is hard at work, constructing concrete conditions that will conform precisely to your suspicions. This is the classic vicious circle. You are utilizing the law of truth – that our thought creates our destiny – in a negative sense. This is how complete untruths are transformed into fact through perpetual doubt and suspicion.

Not knowing the law of truth, human beings continue to doubt with all their might, never noticing that the fruits of their own thinking have materialized in their world.

∽ *There is No One to Blame*

Though your suspicion may be aimed at someone in particular, in reality it has nothing to do with that person – the other party is not responsible for it at all.

Returning to our earlier example, let us say that your husband has indeed had a love affair. Even so, it is not up to you to accuse him. In upsetting your life – and his lover's life as well – he has incurred a debt that must be settled in the course of his own destiny. He will not be able to escape from it. This is not because you or his lover chose to accuse him. In the process of his own awakening to truth, he will eventually have to shoulder responsibility for his own actions.

This is why you are not entitled to blame and judge your husband for his unfaithfulness, nor do you have the right to impugn his character, harass or condemn him. Even if you go to those lengths, it can never ease your sadness or your resentment.

Your husband's infidelity occurred through karmic causes shared by the two of you. If you raise a great fuss and scream for a divorce simply out of emotionalism, it will only add to your problems. It is you who will suffer, and your life that will be thrown into upheaval.

Your present state of mind was not caused by your husband's infidelity. Your husband's infidelity occurred at a point in your destiny when you were meant to come to terms with an issue of your own. It was a moment when a past cause emerged from your subconscious world – a world that you created – in the process of extinguishing itself. That is all it was. If your husband had not been unfaithful, your past cause and effect would have been rectified in another way, perhaps through your child, or your in-laws, or a close friend.

The point is that our past causes are destined to manifest themselves, in some form or other, so that we can focus our attention on truth and deepen our understanding of truth. It brings us an opportunity to cultivate our inner Self. In this sense, one minor doubt can serve as the inducement for us to look into our own mentality and guide ourselves toward truth.

⌔ *See Others as Your Benefactors*

People often seek the cause of their suffering in others. They mistakenly believe that it comes from outside themselves, but this can never be so. The cause was originally projected by their own thought, and so it concerns them alone.

On the surface, it may appear that another person gave rise to the cause. But in fact, they were merely the vehicle for drawing out your problem and letting it manifest itself in this tangible world. In truth, everything stems from your own past consciousness. Other people or members of your family are merely serving as guides for manifesting your past causes in this present world. If, in spite of this truth, you choose to view others as your tormentors – hating them, resenting them and being jealous of them – you will never climb out of your misery. It is crucial to deepen your understanding of this: everything that occurs in your world is the outcome of your thought.

All the people around you have been put there so as to let you encounter truth. Their existence has great value for you, for it is only through them that your spirit has an opportunity for advancement. Without them you would lack the means for bringing out your divinity. You may find some of them lovable, some hateful, some admirable and some distasteful; yet each of them, through their connection with you, has a role to play in guiding you along your path to truth.

Some of these people may have been assigned the role of incurring your hatred; some may be responsible for bringing you sadness or sorrow. If you cherish only the people whose role is to inspire your love, while you hate and dislike those who are assigned with criticizing, blaming and judging you, you are treating the latter unfairly. They did not incur your hatred by choice, or because it brought them any enjoyment. It was your own divine Guide who thoughtfully arranged for them to be placed around you, so that your spirit might evolve.

This makes it all the more necessary for you to appreciate and love those who hate, dislike or blame you – even more than you love those who love you. Their existence is precious to you, for they are your benefactors – guides to your awakening. If you are able to sense this profound intention of the divine, you have understood truth, and are walking the path to spiritual freedom. Soon you will be able to sing life's praises with an untroubled heart. Abundantly overflowing infinite love, happiness and success will surely make themselves known to you, and your life will flourish beyond your highest expectations.

⤳ Convert Your Doubts into Springboards to Truth

In this present-day material world, once we doubt one thing, we soon find ourselves doubting everything. We start having misgivings about our future, society and humanity. We fret about illness, about our children and about our death. There is no end to our doubts and worries.

If you have enough spare time to spend doubting, why not try to live the present moment to the fullest instead? Cut short your doubts this very instant. You are the one who is suffering because of them. Once you remove them from your framework, what relief and freedom you will feel! How innocent, carefree and secure you will become!

What reason could you possibly have for letting doubt eat away at your healthy mind and body? There is a better choice for you: utilize each doubt as a springboard to truth and submit it to the process of your awakening.

Try creating a new and constructive use for the time that you have been squandering on doubt. Spend your mental energy giving yourself words that reinforce truth – words of infinite love, happiness and renewal.[8] To your surprise, you will naturally come to see that doubt is not intrinsic to your nature.

You will look back on it as an illusion, a distorted thought that you once created, nothing more.

Try to have thoughts of appreciation towards the people you are doubtful about. Try believing in your husband, your wife or your children. If you do, you will receive their trust in return.

Let go of your attachment to doubt. Cast it aside without delay. Live each day with a renewed spirit. When these changes take place in you, they will spontaneously take place in those around you, and at the same time you will start believing in yourself.

Happiness is being able to believe in your own truly marvellous qualities. The ability to believe is your most valuable treasure. At the moment when each person believes in his or her divinity, peace will prevail on earth.

May Peace Prevail on Earth.

Chapter 10

YOU CAN PUT
YOUR BELIEFS INTO
PRACTICE

When it comes to spiritual faith, or principles of truth, there are a great many degrees of belief and degrees of practice. There are people who are totally unclear about principles of truth. There are people who are more or less acquainted with these principles, but have doubts about them. There are people who have an understanding of truth, but cannot put it into practice. There are people whose understanding is comprehensive, but take it only as conceptual knowledge and cannot believe it. There are people who simply and spontaneously accept truth, and make efforts to put it into practice, however slightly. There are people who can deeply understand truth and can also put it into practice. And there are people who melt wholly into truth and become living examples of it. Thus we see quite a variety of stages and attitudes, depending on the person.

Many people, though their understanding and belief are extensive, honestly feel that the goals of their faith are too high for their present self to attain.

For example, they believe that they must love others, yet they do not.

They believe that they need to let go of their egos, yet they cannot.

They believe that the past is behind them, yet the past still lives in their hearts.

They believe that they must forgive themselves, but they do not.

Though they believe in condemning the offence and pitying the offender, they condemn the offender.

They believe that they must give their all, yet they do not do this.

They believe that hypocrisy is not good, yet they end up doing hypocritical things.

Though they believe that they should accept whatever comes to them, they cannot.

In this way, most people's heads are filled with things that they earnestly believe in, yet they honestly feel that it is all but impossible to put their beliefs into practice.

Even so, for the beliefs mentioned so far, it is not overwhelmingly difficult for people to comprehend them and strive to put them into practice. This is because, in their hearts, they are clearly satisfied with these things. Their meaning is clear enough for them to be understood, accepted and believed in.

However, when we go one step further, we reach a point where even believing becomes difficult.

For instance, people *try* to believe that unhappiness and suffering do not originally exist, but they cannot believe it.

They *try* to believe that there is originally no such thing as illness, but they cannot believe it.

They *try* to believe that their life unfolds entirely in accordance with their own thinking, but they cannot believe it.

They *try* to believe that, even though the physical body dies, there is, in truth, no such thing as death, and that life continues endlessly. Yet though they try to, they cannot believe it.

And when it comes to the ultimate truth, that human beings are children of God and essentially the same as God, however they may try, a great many people feel that it is far, far beyond them to believe it.

✑ *What You Can Believe, You Can Achieve*

If you believe something but cannot achieve it, the day will surely come when you *will* be able to put your belief into practice. The fact that you believe something means that you will definitely be able to accomplish it someday. Yet the reverse is also true. As long as you are unable to believe something, you will not be able to achieve it.

If you really want to achieve something, you will have to rise above the state of 'not believing' and enter the state of 'believing'. Though it may seem very difficult to convert your belief into action now, you will surely be able to do it someday.

Everything is determined by what you believe and why you believe it. All the conditions and events that come into your life are the manifestations of what you have believed until now, or of what you used to believe. (Of course, this includes things you believed with a past consciousness, before you were born in this world.)

Likewise, things that we do not believe in will not appear in front of us at all. For example, if we cannot believe that our true Self is one with God, our brilliant, godlike nature will definitely not become clear to us. On the other hand, if we grasp the idea that human beings are born from God and have the nature of God, but cannot believe it from our hearts, the fact that we grasp the idea gives us the opportunity of progressing by one step. Understanding the concept assures us of being able to believe it someday. What hinders our belief now is the fact that our surface consciousness is caught up in conventional thinking, or in subconscious attitudes that block our acceptance of it.

◁ *Your Beliefs Will Find Expression*

Though we have been told that human beings, in their original form, are free from illness and misery, wherever we look we see a great many people who are ill, fearful, stricken with pain, or living without hope. The actual circumstances are such that if someone stood up and announced that there is originally no such thing as illness or unhappiness, the majority of people would find it extremely difficult to accept. Even without taking a broad perspective, we would need to look no further than the inner circle of our own family and friends to see an unending stream of illness, misery and suffering. Faced with these conditions, plus the illness and unhappiness that descend upon ourselves, we might find it very hard to go along with the idea that there is no illness, unhappiness or suffering.

The problem is that when people cannot believe something from their hearts and do not try to believe it, those things that they do not believe in will not appear in front of them at all. Thus the true world, which is free from illness and unhappiness, will not reveal itself in front of them. The things we actually believe, and our reasons for believing them, will determine the kinds of things that appear to us, and these are the only things that will find expression in our life.

When asked *What do you believe in?* your answer might be that you believe in illness. Because you believe in illness, illness appears in front of you. Unhappiness and difficulty appear in front of you.

Why do you believe in these things? It is because all of mankind becomes ill, suffers misery and experiences pain. It is because you observe these conditions in the people around you. Here and now, these conditions are not absent. They are present. Rather than believing in what is absent, you believe in what is present in your actual surroundings.

➷ *What You Understand, You Can Believe*

Now let us talk about the next step. Let us consider the people who cannot deny the truth in the words *Illness does not originally exist. Unhappiness and pain do not originally exist.* They cannot deny it because they agree that God is the origin of everything, and that no bad things exist in God. They understand this concept and are satisfied with the truth of it, but they do not believe it from their hearts. They cannot reach that stage of believing, although they are prepared to make efforts toward believing it. People like this can look forward to a bright future, much brighter than if they totally reject the concept.

Such people do not believe in their hearts that there is no illness, trouble or misfortune, but they do not deny it 100 per cent, as do those mentioned earlier. The desire to free themselves from a dark, hopeless life, and to lead a happy one, is blossoming within them. Unconsciously, they are starting to sense that, in some way, their approach has been mistaken. They feel that something in the words *There is originally no illness, unhappiness or hardship* rings true and offers them promise of release.

Yet when they stop and think about it in terms of their actual circumstances, the idea of living without illness and hardship is too fantastic for them to go along with. Even so, the idea attracts them. They believe in the existence of illness, unhappiness and pain but cannot rule out the truth in the idea that illness has no lasting substance.

What, then, do they believe? Just like before, they believe in illness, unhappiness and pain. On the other hand, they can grasp the truth that illness, unhappiness and pain have no original existence at all.

Why do you believe in illness, unhappiness and suffering? It is because these conditions are noticeable in your surroundings.

On the other hand, why do you wish to believe that there is originally no illness, no unhappiness and no suffering? It is because, in the back of your mind, there lurks a fear of illness, an apprehension of misfortune, a loathing of trouble, and it is uncomfortable to live while carrying these ominous feelings around with you.

Perhaps you have been thinking that you would like to find a way out of these fears, but you have not seen a means to accomplish this. When you hear the words *Our original selves are free from illness, unhappiness or trouble,* a feeling of calm comes alive within you. The bright, strong vibration of these true words has filtered into your mind, offering promise of release, though it lasts no longer than a moment.

This is how many people feel. They regard these words of truth as a promising remedy for overcoming fear.

As these people have more opportunity to learn about true principles, they can gradually climb out of their state of inability to believe, and into a state where they are able to believe. When they reach that state, they will find that their frequent occurrences of illness, unhappiness and trouble are starting to diminish. With the power of their past beliefs, they used to draw these conditions toward themselves, but now those old beliefs are changing.

☙ *Your Beliefs Construct Your Experiences*

Human psychology is quite complex and entangled. Our beliefs are a good example of this. Generally speaking, people do not even recognize exactly what it is that they believe. Also, there are different degrees of recognition, depending on each person's state of awareness. Furthermore, their beliefs – and their reasons for believing that way – are gradually changing.

The basic principle, though, does not change. It is a stern, immovable law: in your heart, you can experience only what you believe in. Your convictions have shaped your experiences. This is the essential point.

Your beliefs construct your experiences. I ask you to plant these words in your consciousness, over and over again. If you firmly believe that illness, unhappiness and trouble have no true existence, those very convictions of yours will construct your future experiences without illness, unhappiness or trouble.

From the day we are born until the day we die, life is an unending stream of trouble and misery. Sooner or later, I too will die of illness. This kind of belief constructs a matching kind of experience. Thus, it turns out that people encounter a continuing stream of troubles and miseries as they go through life, and many meet their death in the midst of illness.

ᕦ Mistaken Beliefs Will Fade Away

The things that people believe are deeply rooted, extending far, far back in time. Sooner or later, all of these beliefs have to rise to the surface consciousness or else manifest themselves in our surroundings. Otherwise they would not be able to disappear.

It is important to believe that painful and sad conditions dissipate and vanish when they appear. All we need to do is to think positively that, after those things have vanished, the situation will definitely improve – and keep on believing it. If we consistently think this way, a bright future will open up for us. Just as with our other beliefs, the degree to which we grasp this point and believe it will determine the degree to which our future improves.

If we believe this, what is our reason for believing it? It is because we believe that things are meant to get better. We believe in improvement. The next question is, to what extent do we believe it? Do we believe it 100 per cent? Or 70 per cent? Or 50 per cent? Or 20 per cent? Depending on the depth and strength of our belief, our lives can change significantly.

As various circumstances occur in our lives, each of us responds to those circumstances with a different degree of trust in true principles. When, all of a sudden, you are faced with signs of an illness that you have not anticipated, how do you deal with fear and anxiety? Right away, it would be good if you could think like this: *This is fading away. My past beliefs and past actions are now revealing themselves. They were recorded in my subconscious – and in the earth's collective subconscious – and now they are coming out in the form of this illness. This is not a problem for me. As soon as they come out they are sure to vanish. Thank you, God. May Peace Prevail on Earth.*

Face your situation this way, with firm conviction. For people who are 100 per cent confident that once this condition is gone, it will never reappear, and whose minds are completely at ease and free from any fear or anxiety whatsoever, the future will turn out exactly as they believe.

⌁ *Your Time Will Come*

For those who also believe it, yet maintain a certain measure of doubt and anxiety, the cause of the affliction will disappear partially. Some traces of it will remain, in proportion to the degree of their doubt and anxiety. For example, if the degree of your belief is 70 per cent, the cause of the affliction will be eliminated by 70 per cent, while the remaining 30 per cent of the cause will re-record itself in your subconscious, becoming the seeds of new fears and anxieties over illness.

This process functions according to the natural law that we can experience only the things we believe in. Likewise, in our hearts, we cannot experience things that we do not believe in. Therefore, the best thing would be to believe only in good things, and not to believe in any bad things.

Human beings have built up a huge quantity of negative[9] thoughts and actions (negative 'causes'), starting far, far back in time. A great many of these negative causes are still stored in the human subconscious. Though people may try to believe only in good things, this is not easy, due to the thick layers of negative causes that have piled up in their minds. Another factor is that, although they would like to believe only in good things, people are deeply entrenched in the general thinking of their society, and are overly attached to conventional knowledge. These circumstances are blocking their ability to believe only in good things and true principles.

Those who are able to recognize and believe in true principles without resistance are those whose subconscious contains an abundance of good causes, or good 'recordings' from past worlds. Those who would like to believe in true principles, but cannot, are restricted by the volume of negative causes recorded in their subconscious.

Even so, if a person earnestly and sincerely wishes to know and understand truth, that person will naturally be able to reach a state of believing. If people are indifferent to true principles, they will repeatedly experience futile existences, over and over again. But when your soul is burning to catch hold of truth, and you genuinely try to devote your attention to truth, the time will surely come when you are able to believe in truth with your whole being.

∽ A Steady and Stable Lifestyle

There are also people who seem very enthusiastic about practising the 'fading away' method described above. When difficult, sad or painful things happen in their own lives, or in the lives of others, they immediately say that these things are fading away, and that, through this, their subconscious will be cleansed and in the end things will turn out well. Then they intensely pray for peace on earth.

When I see people like this, I feel much impressed with how deeply the truth has filled their hearts. But then, the same situation comes to them again. So, again, they practise the 'fading away' method and pray for world peace. Yet within a few months' time the same problem arises once again.

For these people, the problem was not 100 per cent eliminated with a single phenomenon. Even though they practised the method intensively, their understanding and belief were less than 100 per cent.

When all is said and done, the best approach would be to take it step by step, slowly but surely. As we go through stages of believing, of not believing, and then of believing again, we gradually move forward.

After all, if human beings could promptly believe in all true principles without hesitation, the miseries, worries and problems of this world would not occur at all, would they? If people could fully believe in high and true principles, and put them into practice without even one per cent of distrust, criticism or indecision, wars would have disappeared long ago, illness would have evaporated, and mankind would have risen to the purest condition of love, peace and happiness.

Even though we may know about true principles and understand them, putting them into practice is the biggest challenge facing a human being. If we absolutely believed in them, the need to put them into practice would not arise, because believing something and putting it into practice are exactly the same thing. Belief is itself an action.

Take, for example, the most fundamental, true principle that human beings are children of God. If you believe this 100 per cent, you will have no difficulty at all putting it into practice, since believing the truth is the same as performing the truth.

When you deeply and spontaneously believe in the true principle that human beings have unlimited health, unlimited health will come pouring forth from your inner Self. Unlimited wisdom will come pouring forth. Even if you have made no particular effort, or studied, or endured, or gone through hardships or mental cultivation, unlimited abilities will come cascading forth.

Though this is an ultimate truth, for the general population it seems all but impossible to extend their belief that far. Even among those who are generally regarded as saints, sages, fine or wonderful people, a 70 per cent ability to believe would be in the upper range. Generally speaking, 30 per cent or so would be about average for people who can believe in the truth. These are people with an abundance of good causes recorded in their subconscious. They could be described as 'spiritually awakened'.

✎ Our Inner Selves Know the Truth

People who have been *trying* to believe are also fine people. And people who believe, but have a hard time putting their beliefs into practice, also come under the category of 'awakened people'.

The most troublesome cases are those who end their lives without even once coming into contact with true principles. It is the same for people who do not try to know about truth, or show no interest in it at all. Even worse is the situation of people who reject or deny true principles. Whatever kind of distress, unhappiness, or illness may take shape in their lives, there seems no way to avoid it. They just resign themselves to it, considering it the normal thing. This is their state of awareness.

In contrast with the helpless situation of these people, I am deeply impressed by those who continue to pray for the peace of mankind. Though many of them are unable to fully believe in its effectiveness, they are trying to do so.

Although, on the physical plane, no one may see or hear what they are doing, on the spiritual plane they are emitting an immensely powerful, purifying light to people who are unaware of truth, do not dare to know truth or are indifferent to it. Even though you do not know their names or have any apparent connection with them, when you pray for peace to prevail on earth you are creating an opportunity for many people to connect with their true selves, however slightly.

Each and every person living in this world already knows the truth in the deepest part of their being. Only their physical consciousness is unawakened to it.

✑ *Happy Are Those Who Can Believe*

I think all of us have had the experience where, through some small occurrence, an old, forgotten memory comes vividly into our mind. If not for that small occurrence, that ancient memory might have remained buried somewhere, never to be recalled during this lifetime.

This is the condition of a large portion of mankind. Just by glancing at the words *May Peace Prevail on Earth* printed on a memo or displayed in a public place, these people have an opportunity to recall the truth of their spiritual identity.

There are so many people still trapped in a world without peace, happiness or harmony, still forced to live amidst illness, hatred or loneliness. When we think about this, we can sense how necessary our daily peace prayers are for supporting each member of humanity. At the same time, our own belief will be strengthened, and a brighter future will span out in front of us.

What, then, will happen to our former self, the 'self' that believed in loving, yet did not love? What will happen to the 'self' that believed in forgiving, yet could not forgive? As we continue converting our thoughts to waves of brilliant light and reading books of truth again and again, we will naturally come to put those beliefs into action without even realizing it.

Until now, you have been trying to show love for others in your words and actions – scolding yourself, coaxing yourself, and half forcing yourself into it. You have tried to do this because you thought you were supposed to; but the door to your heart has been tightly shut. Now, that door has naturally opened. True principles can stream steadily into your heart and be absorbed there. You will come to understand things that have been unclear to you. You will come to sense things that you could not sense before. You will find yourself able to believe what you could not believe before. You will notice changes in yourself, and you will unknowingly bring about changes in humanity.

Happy are those who can believe – but how very many there are who are unable to believe. How noble are those who try to believe! I love them. I unceasingly love the entirety of mankind, and acutely wish for each and every one of us to attain lasting happiness.

The highest, ultimate truth for a human being is that we are all children of God – nothing else. I can naturally believe this without a doubt.

May Peace Prevail on Earth.

PRAYERS OF APPRECIATION
FOR THE EARTH AND
THE ENVIRONMENT

The Way – Truth – is not to be found amidst extraordinary actions. It lies, instead, within the most common and mundane of everyday activities. If we were to take the example of to what we should be thankful for being here today, we might begin by replying that it is the various mechanisms of our bodies continually performing their specified functions that sustain us. According to this line of reasoning, it is our own physical organs that are responsible for keeping us alive here on earth. If this is the case, we should be thankful to our heart, lungs, arms and legs for working continuously on each of our behalves.

There is nothing strange about this feeling of thanks, and I actually think it is a rather obvious feeling of gratitude that we should all practise.

Masahisa Goi, *Lectures on Lao Tzu*[10]

APPRECIATION OF THE SEA

On behalf of mankind, we thank you, divinities in charge of the sea. We thank you, dear sea. Our lives are sustained by you. We thank you from our hearts for your infinite benefits. Please forgive the insolent behaviour of mankind, which does not know your heart.

Please calm the great raging waves that strike shores, wash out beaches and swallow ships. May Peace Prevail on Earth. We thank you, divinities in charge of the sea.

APPRECIATION OF THE EARTH

On behalf of mankind, we thank you, divinities in charge of the earth. We thank you, dear earth. Our lives are sustained by you. We thank you from our hearts for your infinite blessings, that bear, nourish and enliven all lives.

May Peace Prevail on Earth. We thank you, divinities in charge of the earth.

APPRECIATION OF ANIMALS

On behalf of mankind, we thank you, divinities in charge of animals. We thank you, insects, fish and shellfish, reptiles, birds, mammals and all other dear animals. Our lives are sustained by you, and we have prospered through you. We heartily thank you for your infinite benefits. Please forgive the unfeeling behaviour of mankind, which ignores your heart.

May Peace Prevail on Earth. We thank you, divinities in charge of animals.

APPRECIATION OF MOUNTAINS

On behalf of mankind, we thank you, divinities in charge of mountains. We thank you, dear mountains. Our lives are sustained by you. We heartily thank you for your infinite blessings. Please forgive the selfish behaviour of mankind, which does not know your heart.

Please still your heart, that urges our awakening by causing eruptions, explosions and landslides. May Peace Prevail on Earth. We thank you, divinities in charge of mountains.

APPRECIATION OF MINERALS

On behalf of mankind, we thank you, divinities in charge of minerals. We thank you, rocks, stones, coal, petroleum and all other dear minerals. Our lives are daily sustained by you. We heartily thank you for your infinite benefits. Please forgive the irresponsible behaviour of mankind, which does not notice your heart, or which takes such behaviour even while knowing your heart.

May Peace Prevail on Earth. We thank you, divinities in charge of minerals.

APPRECIATION OF FOODS

On behalf of mankind, we thank you, divinities in charge of foods. We thank you, all dear foods. Our lives are sustained by you. Please forgive mankind's selfishness, discontent and lack of appreciation of foods. We heartily thank all foods, the sources of energy that enliven and activate us.

May Peace Prevail on Earth. We thank you, divinities in charge of all foods.

APPRECIATION OF PLANTS

On behalf of mankind, we thank you, divinities in charge of plants. We thank you, grass, flowers, trees and all dear plants. Our lives are sustained by you, and we are comforted by you. We heartily thank you for your infinite blessings. Please forgive the selfish behaviour of mankind, which does not discern your heart.

May Peace Prevail on Earth. We thank you, divinities in charge of plants.

APPRECIATION OF THE PHYSICAL BODY

On behalf of mankind, we thank the physical body.

Each cell that composes my physical body, thank you for enabling me to safely live one more day today. Thank you, all functions, all blood, all bones, all body fluids, all nerves, all muscles, all internal organs and all physical structures. Without this physical body, perfect peace cannot be realized in this world. We respect, love and take good care of the physical body as a holy divine vessel and manifestation.

May Peace Prevail on Earth. May the physical body's divine missions be accomplished.

APPRECIATION OF WATER

On behalf of mankind, we thank you, divinities in charge of water. We thank you, dear water. Without you, we cannot live. Please forgive the foolishness of staining you with the egoism of human beings. We heartily thank you for your existence and functions.

May Peace Prevail on Earth. We thank you, divinities in charge of water. May the divine missions of water be accomplished.

APPRECIATION OF HEAVENLY PHENOMENA

On behalf of mankind, we thank you, divinities in charge of heavenly phenomena. We thank you, rain, wind, snow, clouds, stars and all other heavenly phenomena. Our lives are sustained by you from day to day. Please forgive the insolent behaviour of mankind, which does not know your vast heart.

May Peace Prevail on Earth. We thank you, divinities in charge of heavenly phenomena.

APPRECIATION OF AIR

On behalf of mankind, we thank you, divinities in charge of air. We thank you, dear air. Our lives are sustained by you from moment to moment. Please forgive the foolishness of defiling you with the egoism of human beings.

May Peace Prevail on Earth. We thank you, divinities in charge of air.

APPRECIATION OF THE SUN

On behalf of mankind, we thank you, divinities in charge of the sun. We thank you, dear sun. We are sustained by your energy from moment to moment. Without you, all life forms would be unable to live. We heartily thank you for your limitless blessings.

May Peace Prevail on Earth. We thank you, divinities in charge of the sun.

WORDS OF INFINITE LIGHT

May Peace Prevail on Earth

Infinite Love
Infinite Harmony
Infinite Peace
Infinite Light
Infinite Power
Infinite Wisdom
Infinite Life

May Peace Prevail on Earth

Infinite Happiness
Infinite Flourishing
Infinite Abundance
Infinite Supply
Infinite Success
Infinite Ability
Infinite Possibility

May Peace Prevail on Earth

Infinite Health
Infinite Sparkle
Infinite Renewal
Infinite Freshness
Infinite Refreshment
Infinite Vitality
Infinite Hope

May Peace Prevail on Earth

Infinite Freedom
Infinite Creation
Infinite Expansion
Infinite Dimension
Infinite Development
Infinite Energy
Infinite Gratitude

May Peace Prevail on Earth

Infinite Joy
Infinite Beauty
Infinite Youth
Infinite Good
Infinite Sincerity
Infinite Purity
Infinite Rightness

May Peace Prevail on Earth

Infinite Integrity
Infinite Courage
Infinite Progress
Infinite Betterment
Infinite Strength
Infinite Intuition
Infinite Innocence

May Peace Prevail on Earth

Infinite Forgiveness
Infinite Glory
Infinite Nobleness
Infinite Dignity
Infinite Blessing
Infinite Brightness
Infinite Tolerance

NOTES

1   In this work the terms 'destiny' and 'fate' are used interchangeably.

The term used in the Japanese original is *unmei* (運命). *Un* (運) means 'move' or 'carry' and *mei* (命) means 'life'. Thus *unmei* ('destiny' or 'fate') is the sequence of conditions or events that 'carry' our life.

2   Relating to 'karma', the energy of thought-waves generated by a past consciousness. While there is both 'good karma' and 'bad karma', in this work 'karmic' refers to 'bad karma': the energy of inharmonious thought-waves.

3   Masahisa Goi, 神と人間 *(God and Man)*, Byakko Shuppan, 1953.

4   Mark 2:22.

5   The 'third-dimensional world' refers to the material world. 'Third-dimensional culture', or material culture, is one stage in the evolution of earth. (The next stage will be 'fourth-dimensional culture', or spiritual culture, developed through unchanging principles of peace and harmony.)

6   The world peace prayer, *May Peace Prevail on Earth*, was introduced by Masahisa Goi (1916–80), founder of two international peace organizations: The World Peace Prayer

Society, headquartered in New York, and the Byakko Shinko Kai, headquartered in Ichikawa, Japan.

7   Refer to Appendix I for prayers of gratitude to Nature.

8   Some useful 'words of infinite light' are introduced in Appendix II.

9   Terms such as *positive* and *negative* or *plus* and *minus* are sometimes used to describe the functions of male and female energy or electrical charges. In this translated work, such nuances are not generally intended. *Plus* or *positive* simply connote something favourable or constructive, while *minus* or *negative* connote something unfavourable or destructive.

10   Masahisa Goi, 老子講義 *(Lectures on Lao Tzu)*, Byakko Shuppan, 1963.